CRACKING
THE AMERICA
CODE

This book is dedicated to my parents, who are my gateway to continuity; my wife, who is my present; and my children, who are the key to the future.

My thanks also to Dan and Lary—without whose patience, support, and professionalism this book might not have been and certainly would not have been as it is.

CRACKING
THE AMERICA
CODE

A PLAN FOR GETTING
US BACK ON TRACK

JOHN KRUBSKI

www.theamericacode.com

email: krubski@theamericacode.com

ISBN 978-0-9827554-4-0

A Buoy Point Media Production

Buoy Point Media
26 Schoolhouse Road
PO Box 433
Waccabuc, NY 10597

www.buoypoint.com
email: publisher@buoypoint.com

CONTENTS

PART TWO

How the America Code Plays Out Here and in the World

FOREWORD

As this book is being written, it is 2012. America faces unprecedented challenges and a future for which some say it is unprepared. Are Americans up to the challenge? Do we have the "juice" to make it through another twenty-five years at the head of the global table, much less another hundred? Do we have the guts to tough it out for even a decade in a world where others are allegedly in the ascendancy? Will we become the creatures of our social, political, or economic "betters"?

Some say that, at 250 years, we have had a great run...it is time to face the facts. We have grown arrogant. We have grown lazy. We have lost our way. We have overextended ourselves beyond our capabilities. They say that we now need to take our lead from others on the planet, others better equipped to lead the world community where it "should" go. They say we need to accept the view that America is a quaint anachronism built on outdated notions, that it is a fading star, and that our once-vaunted Constitution is an increasingly irrelevant document not hip or glib enough for these sophisticated modern times.

I say this is balderdash! Poppycock! There are two intensely underappreciated expressions that deserve to be reenergized for this particular discussion and perhaps beyond. If you believe or subscribe to any of the above, then you obviously don't get America or Americans. You clearly don't appreciate how America evolved. Most significantly, you just don't understand that America and Americans are fundamentally, congenitally, and, I believe, genetically different than the lot we left behind. What we have created here will never be the same as the roots from which we sprang because we actively and purposely severed our ties with those roots for a set of consistent reasons. Moreover, archetypal Americans, as I define them later in this book, continue to swell our numbers, not because we are like the rest of the world but specifically because we are not like any other nation on the planet.

I do not personally subscribe to the position that defines the phrase "American exceptionalism" as implying that America or Americans are better and other nations are not as good in an abstract continuum of national perfection. I do believe that the American people and the idea of America are exceptional in the sense that we are different from other nations, for that we undeniably and demonstrably are.

If you want to evaluate our ability to do better than hang on, you really need an in-depth, no-holds-barred understanding of what makes America America and what makes Americans Americans: what causes us to make the decisions we make and to value what we value. That is the subject and the purpose of this book.

I believe that the key to our future lies in having a better understanding of this fundamental American ethos. As a professional communicator and persuader, I also believe, because I have seen it work so well so often, that this same understanding makes it possible to better communicate with, sell to, manage, persuade, and motivate Americans of all stripes in a wide range of situations and circumstances.

The first step in cracking what I call the *America Code* is recognizing that the word "Americans" itself is a generalization. As such, it describes only a portion of the American reality it tries to embrace. Believing or implying that all Americans are exactly alike is akin to assuming that every tree ever grown is a duplicate of its predecessor, neighbor, or successor. That kind of consistency applies as little to our nation as it does to the typical forest. A tree may be a tree, but every forest is made up of an immense diversity of trees.

In this book, I will introduce the idea of American diversity in a different light—not one based on age or sex or national origin or any of the traditional senses in which we generally understand diversity but in a more fundamental and a more functional sense. Based on an original piece of research that I have conducted for more than twenty years, The Index of What Matters Most™, and more than 35,000 participants in that research model, "Americans" fall into three broad segments: *Foundational Americans, Situational Americans,* and *Archetypal Americans.*

Why is it a good idea to reframe the conversation about who we are and how we got here? Haven't we talked about that enough already? The future of America will not be decided by how we tackle any one, or four, or a hundred issues, no matter how critical these may seem. America is about who we are much more than it is about *what* we do. The future of America will be decided by how well we understand *who* "we" are, how we got here, and how effectively we deploy the same mechanics that have defined us as a nation and a people for more than 250 years as we go forward.

Who will that "we" be in the long haul so that we can still be Americans living in America? I believe the answer to that question and to figuring out a strategy for getting us back on track, as a country and as individuals, lies in understanding the unique formula that I call the *America Code*.

PART ONE

The America Code — What It Is and How We Have Evolved It

"American" is more nature than nationality. It is coming home to a place we've never been before.

SECTION I

What Makes an American American?

YOU CAN QUALIFY TO CALL YOURSELF AN AMERICAN based on one of three criteria: *situational, foundational,* or *archetypal.*

The easiest way to be "American" is *situational*—to have the good fortune to find yourself physically in America at any particular moment. This definition embraces first-generational (and beyond) citizens of American birth, along with immigrants—both legal and illegal—of variable seniority. You qualify merely by being in the right place at the right time.

You qualify to be described as a *Foundational American* if you can prove to be one of the millions of the "posterity" specifically referred to in the Preamble to the US Constitution. That document was written so as to secure for you, as heirs of the Foundational Americans, "the blessings of liberty." Taken literally, then, any child of a child of a child (etc.) of one of the signers of the Constitution (as well as the population they represented or the progeny of any person living in America at that time) could be thought of as a Foundational American—participating in the creation of the nation directly or by heredity.

But America has always been less interested in status based on heredity (the specific evil from which we liberated ourselves through the Revolutionary War) than it has been in a status based on substance. The third type of American status is the one that most intrigues (as well as describes) me and that forms the core of this book: the *Archetypal American.* Archetypal Americans may fall into one of the other two types of American typologies as well, but there is something fundamentally different about them—because who they are is not circumstantial but elemental and how they get to be Americans is active rather than passive.

There is also much to be said about the fact that the people who first landed on these shores and settled here (as opposed to those who were simply passing through) were every bit like the Archetypal Americans who have been here only a short time and are on their way to becoming citizens of this country. For that matter, Archetypal Americans, as we will later see, may not even be in America yet—although they are, in fact, elemental Americans in every sense of the word but procedural.

America is not merely a place or an idea. It is a developing, evolving dynamic. There always have been, are now, and will always be naturally disposed Archetypal Americans available and willing to participate in and contribute to America's creation, evolution, and regeneration. Whether those Americans originate in Argentina, Poland, Bangladesh, or wherever circumstances may currently find them—and whether they have as yet reached these shores or not, these are the people of whom we speak when we talk about "Americans" and the product of their labors, "America," in all the many meanings and nuances of the words.

CHAPTER 1

Natural Causes and Actions vs. Circumstances

IN THE CHAPTERS THAT FOLLOW, we are not simply going to restate the well-worn and presumptive propositions that America is a "nation of nations." Neither are we going to maintain that everything can be explained by the understanding that we are a land of immigrants. Both examples would only be yet another attempt to explain the substance of the America Code by pointing to its most obvious symptoms. Our goal here is to get well below the obvious.

Fair warning: To get the most from this book, you would be best served by opening yourself to consider (not necessarily accept—at least for now) the possibility that what makes Americans Americans does not merely require that they find themselves in the physical space called America. At the same you might consider accepting the notion, no matter how conditionally, that being in America, even after multiple generations, does not necessarily make someone American—at least not in the quintessential sense—any more than being in school makes someone a scholar or being part of a sports team makes someone an athlete.

At the same time, I believe that being an American is the by-product of actions *you* take and decisions *you* make. It doesn't just wash over you like some sort of gentle rain of Liberty. Becoming and being an Archetypal American involves an initial choice and a series of actions that support that choice over time.

CHAPTER 2

The Element of Choice

AMERICA IS THE ONLY COUNTRY ON THE PLANET where the majority of the citizenry are here because of a conscious act of choice. This country has been populated almost exclusively either by direct action or as a consequence of the direct action of others. In other words, we are who we are and America is what it is not because of chance and accident but because of conscious decisions repeated over time.

The latest available census figures report on a fascinating outcome of this choice factor: when given an opportunity to define their "national origin," more than 92 percent of responding Americans chose some designation other than "American." Clearly, even after as much as ten or more generations, most of us realize that we are Americans because we chose to come here. We are not Americans by default or circumstance. We are Americans because Germans, Irishmen, Englishmen, Mexicans and Spaniards, Frenchmen, Italians, Poles, Chinese, Cambodians...and on and on and on made the decision to leave everything behind and head across the great and dangerous "pond" to get here. That same choice is still being made by new generations of archetypal Americans.

This makes us different as a nation in a unique way. Go to any country in Europe, the Far or Middle East, Asia, Central or South America. In virtually every case the population of each is predominantly (more than 85 percent) made up of a homogeneous people whose roots go back a very, very, very, very long way. There are several obvious exceptions. Australia was populated by choice, but not necessarily the choice of the settler. Mexico's population is a strong combination of indigenous peoples (not from any single Indian nation, but from many) intermingled with immigrant Spaniards. There is also the matter of "made-up" countries that were created as a political convenience but have proven largely insupportable in practice.

Then there's France, about whose makeup we are not allowed to know as the French passed a law during the Third Republic (1871–1940) that forbids asking people about or recording their "alleged" national origins. So it's a little difficult to know what, precisely, makes a French person French.

The fact of making a choice to come to America is not as interesting as the implications of such a choice. On the one hand, it says a lot about the person making such a decision. My parents, for example, traveled across three continents and four countries on a ten-year journey finally to make their way to these shores.

Coming to America has never been an easy trip, and in many cases it still isn't. I believe it is such a trial, indeed, as to filter out the less adventurous and committed, to thwart those with less initiative and perseverance, and to favor people who are driven to dare against the odds. Those who make the journey are fundamentally different from those who stay behind. In a very real sense, making the decision to leave home and travel here and then sustaining that decision to a successful arrival is a literal rite of passage— every bit as meaningful and defining as any other rite of passage whose achievement marks a person as distinct and exceptional relative to those who don't begin or complete the exercise.

CHAPTER 3

A Homecoming

OVER THE YEARS, I have met literally thousands of American immigrants— people from all walks of life, from every economic class, and from a wide array of home countries. I love hearing them talk about this country as they see it. "What a country!" is consistently the most common phrase I hear. That simple exclamation speaks volumes.

As eloquent as they are, the words aren't nearly as exhilarating as the energy and the body language that go with them—a broad toothy grin and guileless delight. It has never failed to reenergize and inspire me to see such unbridled and unrepressed joy associated with being in America, much less actually having achieved citizenship. These people don't apologize for being Americans; they revel in it.

So...how does it come to pass that people who have come here recently seem to be more connected to and more energized by the notion of America and everything for which it stands the instant they set foot here than by the country from which they have come? A pessimistic assessment might be that they haven't been here long enough to have seen the bad with the good. But that would miss the point because this response comes as energetically from recent arrivals to our shores as from immigrants who have been here for decades. True, after a generation or two or three, the enthusiasm isn't quite as strong as for new arrivals. I don't believe it fades or evaporates; it simply takes a less front-and-center place in our lives. We tend to take what America is for granted. The cure for this is simply to spend time with those who are only too happy to remind us how great a place America is...lest we lose sight of the reality.

What is it about America that so excites and delights first-generation immigrants? What makes them so happy to be here? It is only over the past few years that I have finally figured out from whence this positive joyful energy emanates. To paraphrase an old John Denver song, they are "coming home to a place [they've] never been before...." They are coming home to the ideal that comes as naturally to them as breathing. Coming to America is, for most people who make the journey, a true homecoming.

I have come to believe that these people were born "American"—in essence if not in geography. There is something fundamental, an internal predisposition that connected them with the American essence at the moment they were born. The moment they arrive on these shores, they (and all their predecessor immigrants) understand that they are "finally" where they belong. They are not Americans because they came here—they came here because they are (and always have been in some elemental way) Archetypal Americans by nature.

CHAPTER 4

The Genetic Compass

IF IMMIGRATING TO AMERICA IS A PASSAGE OF HOMECOMING, then how do we know which way to head when we leave *back there* and how do we know that we have arrived *here*? I suppose you could attribute all that to literature, exposure, and maps. But that would be missing the key ingredient. Of all the people in the world who have known about America and what it represents, why is it that only a small minority from each country (except perhaps for the Irish, as much as 20 percent of whom left the mother country and headed west) choose to make the transit? More significantly, why is it that those who do make the journey unerringly find their way to the one place that "fits" who and what they are all about?

Salmon and sea turtles unerringly return to the place at which they were conceived—even though they technically did not exist at that moment. They manage this difficult exercise no matter how much of the globe they may wander through some sort of genetic collective memory—a biological compass that points to "home" as unfailingly as conventional magnets point to the magnetic North Pole.

My success or failure as a professional persuader depends largely on the ability to discern the difference between what is basic and fundamental about a group of people (usually called the "target segment") and what is circumstantial and changeable. Over the course of my thirty-year career, I have looked inside the minds of literally thousands of Americans one-on-one. I have polled and surveyed tens of thousands of others. With that much exposure to and examination into why people make the decisions they make and why they value what they value, I've developed a finely tuned intuition about what really drives values and behavior in human beings. Over time, I've learned to discern the fundamental mechanisms that bind one group of people and separate them from others. More often than not, the underlying truth cannot be empirically defined and statistically demonstrated—yet it is still there.

For a marketer like me, tapping into that well of insight and perspective is an essential part of my ability to communicate with and persuade people to a particular point of view or an action.

Americans follow the same principle. We are drawn to a place that has become the wellspring of the values that underlie the visible markers of the America Code. Perhaps the coded direction is as simple as "beyond the horizon."

In the first place, "beyond the horizon" points primarily toward North America whether you begin in Europe, Africa, or Asia. But the idea of "beyond the horizon" is more than a geographic pointer. If you have ever been on an ocean, you understand that sense of a horizon without landmarks, without certainty, with a hint of infinity, that calls on something deep down inside some people that is not shared by others. The very notion of traveling to a destination that you cannot see draws only those with the courage, the inventiveness, the optimism, and the industry to set off seeing nothing and yet clearly expecting to find a better place than that from which you departed.

The American genetic compass tells those of us who make the journey not only where to head, but also defines the nature of the company of those coming along for the ride.

CHAPTER 5

Not the Lot We Left Behind

LATELY, IT HAS BECOME INCREASINGLY FASHIONABLE in some circles to talk about how much America and Americans can learn from the more established countries of Europe and Asia. For some there still exists a sense that America is somehow yet untried, unseasoned, and inexperienced in the way of more sophisticated nations. Apparently, there are Americans among us who yearn to mirror the values and social systems of our distant cousins across the sea.

Now, here's the problem. America was founded by people who wanted to leave that lot behind. They were the *disenfranchised diligent optimists* who did not fit neatly with the primeval European tribal model. The government and society in Europe, Asia, and much of the rest of the world are still heavily entrenched in the idea that the group (the tribe or the country; the collective, if you like) is more important than the individual. In that model and for the sake of the common good of the group, there are natural leaders. More often than not that leadership is either literally or functionally hereditary. Everyone in the group is harnessed to the survival and betterment of the group.

On the one hand, the primeval tribal model (even extended to a latter-day socialistic society) ensures everyone a place in the tepee. On the other hand, that seat is more likely than not to be assigned by the "betters" (once the chieftains) who are expected and empowered to make such decisions of place and placement. The underlying theme of the model and the implicit contract it involves is this: "You are nothing, you have nothing, you are no one, until someone in a position over you (the king, the chief, the lordling, the master) gives you what they decide you should have. At that point, you are expected to bend a knee and utter an appropriate thank you."

I believe that is the fundamental separator between those who make the journey to America and the lot who stays behind. Americans do not fancy bending the knee, bowing, or being graciously thankful for something we believe to be our natural due and that we can very well achieve on our own. It is no accident that our Declaration of Independence specifically decrees the existence of "certain unalienable rights" and goes on to enumerate them as the right to life, the right to liberty, and the right to pursue (not necessarily guarantee and possess) happiness.

In the first place, we clearly believe that the rights come from the Creator and not from any individuals or organizations on earth. Aside from reaffirming that the United States was founded on a platform of religious principles that recognized an authority higher than that of the state, the Declaration of Independence also basically argues that one man is not beholden to another man for such fundamental rights.

In the second place, we tend to vastly underappreciate what that short list of rights really represents. It lies at the core of our concept of individual liberty. The Declaration of Independence establishes every person's unconditional right to his or her own life. At a time when the monarch could arbitrarily condemn citizens to death for a variety of "crimes and offenses against the crown," that was more than a novelty—it was a social game-changer. Similarly, the unalienable right to life was a protection from the capriciousness of the rights of your "betters" to decide whether you would live or die.

The most illuminating item in the list of Declaration rights is the right to the "pursuit of happiness." It was not the document's or the new American society's job to provide each citizen with happiness, but rather to ensure that all citizens had the right to provide that happiness for themselves—the ultimate guarantee of earning the fruit of their individual industriousness.

Then there's the word "unalienable." In Jefferson's original draft notes, it's "inalienable"—so there has been a lot of discussion about the difference between the two. Some say that "inalienable" implies that a person can give up such rights, trade them in for something else. "Unalienable," on the other hand, says the rights cannot be severed (given up or given away)—neither by the person possessing them nor by anyone else.

I believe that Jefferson's original use of the word "inalienable" gives us a bit of a clue as to the origin of the list of rights in the Declaration. One nuance of Jefferson's original choice of word is that inalienable rights can be transferred, but only with the consent of the person possessing those rights.

That, I think, is the difference between those who make the journey to individual liberty and those who stay behind. We are genetically incapable of letting go of what we feel is intrinsically part of being human, and we trust our own initiative. They are predisposed to evaluate and trade off such fundamental elements in favor of a guaranteed entitlement. The difference is either easy or impossible to adequately explain. It's a lot like buying a boat—if you ask me to explain why I need a boat, you are already unequipped to understand the explanation.

CHAPTER 6

A Nation by Nuances, Halves, and Trichotomies

ARE ALL AMERICANS THE SAME? Are we a seamlessly homogeneous, consistent people from the first million to the final 312th million of us? Were we ever one single cookie-cutter look-alike nation? The answer is a resounding...no!

Most often when we use the term "Americans" we don't think deeply about what we're describing. At one level, the expression applies to Americans of every stripe and political leaning, every generational nuance and social status, and the list of presumptions goes on and on. Presumption, actually, is the very root of the problem. "Americans" tends to include everybody under one roof and in a single cohort. It's a singular prototypical stereotype that assumes all Americans are not only equal but also the same. It's just about the broadest generalization possible. As such, it works only in theory.

In practice, we clearly perceive two types of Americans. The first type is "Us!"—I and all like-minded, reasonable, intelligent, caring, and thoughtful people. Every time we seek universal agreement for our beliefs, we immediately discover that there are also "They!" out there—those incredibly ignorant, recalcitrant, obstreperous, disagreeable, unreasonable, or uncaring individuals who just can't see the truth as we so readily do!

I have been on this planet long enough to appreciate, particularly in politics but also in life in general, that most human interactions as well as "the truth" are relative propositions. What is clear and unequivocal to some is almost invariably fuzzier or even unequivocally wrong to others. In a number of ways, America is at least a nation of dichotomies. What's even more fascinating is that the dichotomies appear to almost perfectly divide us into what are two measurably different sets of Americans—and it's been that way from the very beginning. According to estimates[1] by some historians, about 45 percent of the colonists actually favored independence. The rest were either Loyalists or chose not to be involved. The idea of American independence started out as a 50/50 from the outset. As we will later see (under the heading "How Half of America Is Coded to Disagree"), in poll after poll just about half of America disagrees with the other half of America on an incredibly wide range of issues and questions.

For me, at least, this helps to explain why Job One for George Washingon was, more often than not, pleading with the troops not to run off home after their ninety-day enlistment expired. George had few illusions about the commitment of most of his troops to the cause of independence, observing that "after the first emotions are over," those who were willing to serve from a belief in the "goodness of the cause" would amount to little more than "a drop in the Ocean."[2] He was correct. As 1776 progressed, many colonies were compelled to entice soldiers with offers of cash bounties, clothing, blankets, and extended furloughs or enlistments shorter than the one-year term of service established by Congress.

It would be nice if America could be understood merely in terms of a dichotomy—a simple matter of two American values systems. It would be nice, but that kind of simplification causes more misunderstandings than it resolves. To understand the great American dynamic, you have to take it beyond the notion of a bifurcated society.

In his history of the Gallic Wars, Julius Caesar observed *in omnia Gallia in partes tres divisa est.*[3] He was describing ancient France and noting that it was "on the whole... divided into three parts." America and Americans are a bit more complicated. Two types of *trichotomies* are required for a full understanding of how the nationality and the society function.

The first American trichotomy is fundamental. It defines on the basis of status three different types of "Americans"—Foundational, Situational, and Archetypal.

Foundational Americans are those who were present for the process of the country's foundation and took a direct part in achieving independence from England and constituting the new United States of America as well as their descendants. You might also extend that designation to the waves of immigrants, although (a little recognized fact) there was virtually no immigration to the United States between 1790 and 1830. The heavy waves of European immigrants arrived between 1840 and 1930—first German, then Irish and a slightly lesser number of English in the latter waves.

The second American status group is *Situational Americans* (which includes many of the progeny of the Foundational Americans—as well as many of their nonparticipating contemporaries) who became and continue to become Americans through the simple act of being in America. Situational Americans do not necessarily share the fundamental values or traits of Foundational Americans—although they may well do so. In this sense, Situational American status extends to indigenous people who had America thrust on them as well as those African-Americans who were transported here against their will.

The third American status group making up the fundamental American trichotomy is *Archetypal Americans*. Archetypal Americans share the same values systems possessed by Foundational Americans. They possess the genetic Americanisms we will discuss further in this book. Moreover, Archetypal Americans may not actually be in America—yet! As I have come to appreciate, they are Americans by nature and reflect the same approach to life as did the Foundational Americans. These are the people for whom coming to America is more of a homecoming than anything else. Whether they get here or not, they naturally "get" America and all for which it stands.

That brings us to the second and most fascinating American trichotomy— an operational trichotomy based on distinct and definable values systems and the way they play out in behaviors in the polling booth, marketplace, and working environment. The understanding of this particular trichotomy evolved from original research and a proprietary research methodology— The Index of What Matters Most™—which, over a number of separate segmentation studies, pointed to an innovative way of understanding why Americans decide what they decide and value what they value differently. We will dive more deeply into the concept behind these insights in "Eight American Cultureographies" later in this book. For the moment, let's look at the operational American trichotomy in broad strokes.

Based on input from more than 35,000 respondents to the Index of What Matters Most™, America divides into three operating values systems: proactive, inactive, and reactive.

An estimated 44 percent of Americans are fundamentally proactive. They have agendas. They take initiative. They DO! Clearly, they also fall all along the political spectrum, but they are the just-under-50 percent of the population that provides the dynamism and the energy by means of which America evolves.

An estimated 46 percent of Americans are quintessentially inactive. They do not participate. They do not precipitate. They do not activate. This does not mean that they do not have a role at any given moment or under any particular circumstance—but that role will be assigned to or required of them by mechanisms initiated by the proactive part of the population. If you find yourself questioning the scale of inactives in our population, consider this: in most of our presidential elections (the number is decidedly lower in off-year elections), a reasonably consistent average of 46 percent of Americans do not vote! It was, in fact, the serendipitous correlation between this number and the total percentage of inactives in The Index of What Matters Most model that triggered the ultimate insights in this chapter.

If you've been keeping up with the arithmetic, that leaves about 10 percent of Americans unaccounted for. In our model, the remaining 10 percent are reactive. Think of them as people who generally fly under the radar until something triggers either fear or anger that overcomes their natural inertia. Reactives are the so-called swing vote that comes out in response to some issue or another in every election. As we will later discover (see "A Dynamic Sociopolitical Imbalance"), what keeps America on a centrist keel is the rectifying contribution that reactive Americans make to continually unbalancing the entrenched sociopolitical partisans.

CHAPTER 7

National Characters of the Foundational Americans

OVER THE CENTURIES, individuals who share the America Code have been drawn here like bees to fields of flowers. They have contributed to, reinforced, and refined a system and a set of values that were laid down by the initial foundational Americans.

What America ultimately became is largely the product of the initial national characters that contributed to its original establishment and that so eloquently articulated the social and political idea under which we now live.

It is important to remember that the members of each nationality that made the journey are likely to have been different from the members of that same nationality that stayed behind. It takes a special kind of person to stop complaining, take on the challenge, and stick with it through the act of leaving behind everything they know in order to start over again where there is nothing known except faith, hope, and adventure. As we look at the different national characters that made up America, we need to keep in mind that the very act of emigrating from their countries and immigrating to America means that the newcomers had a lot more in common with one another than they did with those they left behind.

While I am very much a fan of the "latest" or "cutting edge" in most things, I also appreciate the value of contemporaneous accounts when it comes to dealing with things historical. Given that kind of thinking, I was lucky to find a cohesive account of most of the national characters that made up the first chapters of the story of America—mostly from a single consistent source. More importantly, that point of view comes from a book written in 1881. The date is ideally situated roughly a century after the writing of the American Constitution and roughly a century before the present day.

The book in question is *Ireland Among the Nations; or the Faults and Virtues of the Irish Compared with Those of the Other Races,* written by the Reverend J. O'Leary, DD, and published by the Irish National Publishing House in Boston in 1881. The Reverend O'Leary was writing at a time when America was defined but also fresh as a member of the world community. His interest, and ours, coincide in that he talks about most of the nations that make up the biggest part of America.

The Reverend clearly had a lot of energy and intensity in describing the group closest to but other than his own. Remember that in the late nineteenth century, the relationship between Protestant England and Catholic Ireland was not a happy one. Moreover, most Irish could point to centuries of suffering largely inflicted on them and sustained by the members of the ruling English gentry in the land of Eire.

THE ENGLISH

The English are, at once, a proud, vain, haughty, and insolent people. There is, further, a pampered set of people, called the aristocracy, whose pride is lifted up to the skies, and whose vanity swelleth infinitely into space...they devour the substance of the people and dream that they are of a purer blood and a higher caste than the mass of human kind.

But the vast mass of the English nation is a mighty multitude of toil, self-reliance, patience, and endurance.... united with this is a self-respect and a self-reliance which are the father and mother of self-importance, if not haughtiness.... the English people at home are candid, frank to bluntness, unforgetful of their words, promises, and contracts, truthful when self-interest does not interfere, and bountiful when self-safety is secured. The brains of the average Englishman are solid and sensible rather than brilliant and intellectual; his will is firm and defiant, but, when broken, knows no resurrection.

O'Leary's view of the French was, understandably, a great deal more affirmative than his view of the British aristocracy as, on numerous occasions, the repressed Irish looked to France as a source of aid and comfort in their long-suffering attempt to rid themselves of the burden of the English royal yoke.

THE FRENCH

There has not been a nation so completely successful in swamping the individual as the 'Grand Nation' of France. Whatever he enters into— and everything he enters into he does so with an intense energy—must first of all be for France. If it is war, it must redound to the glory or aggrandizement of France; if it is religion, it must be the national religion.... all France is incorporated like the limbs of a human body, so that, if one member rejoices, all the members rejoice with it; and if one member suffer, all the members suffer.... It is no wonder that the enthusiastic Frenchman looks on France as beautiful—the land of his love, his fatherland, his church, his household, and home.... Not less remarkable than the homogeneity of France is its steady and stern adherence to principle.

France is the only nation I know of to take up arms for a speculative theory. It would almost declare war to prove the truth or a mathematical problem.... this intelligent, mathematical, excitable, and impressionable people has been the friend of oppressed nationalities the world over. They stood bravely by Washington, and have left the names of Lafayette and Rochambeau as household words to Americans. Many a time they fought and bled on Irish soil for luckless Ireland. There has never been an oppressed nationality that did not have the sons of France fighting in its ranks.

O'Leary was amazed by the industriousness, isolationism, and thriftiness of the Germans he encountered.

THE GERMANS

The Germans are a brave, quiet, and persevering people, and make up by patient dint for their slowness and stolidity. A unity of language has bound them into a kind of nation within a nation in this country [America], so that of all the races they are among the slowest to be naturalized. They are remarkable for their industry, and the unity and allegiance with which they cling to each other. It is almost incredible what an enormous amount of lager-beer saloons they support in this country, and it is astounding what an extraordinary amount of beer is consumed....

Their course appears to be westward, where they can find cheap lands, and thus satisfy an amazing cupidity for the ownership of real estate. One finds the pioneer of the far West an American or an Irishman, among bears and Indians; while safely in the distance a German saloon-keeper awaits the return of the adventurers to deal out drinks, collect the money, and attend to real estate. It surpasses belief how cheaply they can live, and it is incomprehensible how tenaciously they can hold on to money.

Then, of course, are O'Leary's own, the sons of Eire—who, while they only began to arrive on our shores after 1840, have made an impact on the character of the country by their sheer numbers.

THE IRISH

The wild music, the deep pathos, the somber melancholy, the fiery spirit, and the magic genius of Irish bards and Druids had irresistible fascinations for the Irish race. Not less influential was the power of Irish chieftains, especially in time for war; for the Irish, like the Gauls, were always a warlike people, and, after the gifts for their gods, yearned for nothing so much as the glories of the battle-field.

There was, besides, in the homes of the ancient Irish, an inviolable hospitality. The stranger and the friend, the relative and the enemy, were sacred within the Irish home.... Naturally faithful to their obligations, and warmly attached to their friends, they detested what was mean, what was foul, what was unnational and unnatural; and as good works and righteousness bring peace, the land of Eri [ancient Ireland] was a land of joy. Hence the Irish love of song, minstrelsy, and music.... It would be difficult to decide whether the Christian Irish race has clung with greater tenacity to its religion or its nationality; nor does it matter much, for both religion and nationality have been fellow-sufferers, and have given mutual aid and comfort to each other in the darkest hours of Ireland's gloom.

The core, then, of the American character is a rich blend. From the English and the Irish comes a healthy dislike for the haughty and pretentious and a tendency toward the blunt. From the French, an irrepressible desire for liberty and the free flow of ideas and principles, even though those ideals were mainly of and from the French aristocracy of the time—at least that part of the aristocracy that supported our cause against the English monarch. The French of the colonial period had a well-deserved reputation for siding with the underdog of the day—a trait we continue to exhibit in the twenty-first century.

The foundational Germans, who today still make up nearly one in six American family trees, gifted us with frugality, a level-headed practicality, and a strong sense of community—which was echoed and reinforced by the Irish among us.

It can be said frankly and without fear of contradiction that subsequent waves of immigrants from the nations that followed consisted mainly of individuals and families who shared those same fundamental values and who, in turn, each contributed their version of them to America.

CHAPTER 8

The American National Character

IN NOTING THAT AMERICANS FOCUS ON THE PRACTICAL, Alexis de Tocqueville, the French aristocrat and social commentator, observed that our passions, wants, education—everything—"unite in drawing the native of the United States earthward"—in grounding us in the things that we can control.

There are three key elements that distinguish the American character.

We have a tendency to action over complaint. We are tireless workers in our own cause. We have a low tolerance for things we find annoying, distressing, inappropriate, or otherwise unacceptable. Rather than rejoicing in haranguing ourselves and others about this dismal state of affairs, we tend to get off our seats and do something about it. That is the core of the immigration gene.

We have a tendency to naiveté and soft-heartedness. We fundamentally believe that everyone is like us. We expect that others will "naturally" act as we would. We enter into contracts and agreements expecting all others to honor commitments. We believe that everyone is as industrious and as well-intentioned as we are. In a sense, the naiveté comes from our roots as a society of the people, by the people, and for the people. Monarchies tend to be more sophisticated and hardened by their sense of history—not to mention the struggles of ascending to and hanging onto power over generations.

We have a tendency to reinvention. On the one hand, we have an extremely short national memory. We forget wrongs quickly. We also repeat errors because we don't track our history. We more often than not forget why things are done the way they have always been done so we go ahead and make them new again—often regardless of whether they truly need reinvention or not. On the other hand, nothing so suits us as something we have created to meet our own peculiar needs as we perceive them at a particular moment in time.

These key national characteristics contributed to making our history different from those of other countries. They will also continue to keep us on track in the future. Time and time again, one group or another in America agitates for some new revolution. Apparently, these folks don't have an adequate appreciation for who and what we Americans are. As it is, we, among all nations of the planet, are the one least likely to ever experience a real revolution. I say a "real revolution" because our original "revolution" was not against "our" government so much as against a government externally imposed upon us. The American Revolution was, more properly, the American Separation.

Because pretty much every American can have a piece of America all their own, no matter how small, we haven't had a revolution since then—that is, unless you consider the South's secession a revolution. It is unlikely that we ever will have another revolution in America—at least as long as those who had been disenfranchised elsewhere continue to have opportunities and possibilities here. With all Americans having the freedom to do their own thing, particularly on the economic front, de Tocqueville's observation of more than 150 years ago is likely to continue being the state of things in America, for, as he said,

> *I know of nothing more opposed to revolution than commercial mores. In a constitutional and peaceful democracy…love of wealth directs men principally toward industry. Industry…can prosper only with the aid of very regular habits. It is the very violence of their desires that renders the Americans so methodical. It troubles their souls but arranges their lives.… In America everyone works to live, or has worked, or was born of people who worked. The idea of work as a natural and honest condition of humanity is…offered to the human mind on every side.*

CHAPTER 9

A Basic Decency

IN RECENT TIMES, America has been called by some a "cruel country." Obviously, those critics lack an understanding of history, both ours and that of the world "out there." Certainly, between institutional slavery and the Indian wars, Americans have done cruel things at more than one point in our history. Unfortunately, in those moments all we demonstrate is that which we have in common with most of the rest of the world. National cruelty is not an American invention by any means.

However, we left most of that behind as a national policy at least a hundred years ago. The same can't be said for much of the rest of the world. The Russians invented the idea of concentration camps in the eighteenth century. We, the Spanish, and the British used them in the nineteenth and early twentieth centuries. The Nazis perfected the idea half way into the twentieth century. The Japanese took the concept to extremes of cruelty in the Second World War.

Genocide, the most diabolical cruelty of all, was practiced in the twentieth century not only by Hitler and the Nazis in Germany but also by the Japanese on an unprecedentedly personal scale. In China, the communists under Mao Zedong killed somewhere between 50 and 80 million of their own between 1949 and 1969. Stalin in the Soviet Union dispatched more than 23 million "enemies of the state." The Italians under Mussolini had a very poor record in North Africa and at home against their own enemies of the state.

Lesser known are such atrocities as the massacre of an estimated 8 million Africans by the Belgians under King Leopold II between 1886 and 1908. France left its own trail of cruelty in places such as Vietnam and Algeria. Similar indictments can be laid at the feet of the British in India. The list of demonstrably cruel countries is horrendously long and includes the ultimate crimes against humanity continuing well into the twentieth century.

If America can be accused of being a cruel country, it stands in very fine company indeed. Instead, we are, if anything, one of the more decent nations on earth. One of the most valuable things we have brought to the world is a nationalized sense of decency in nature, in spirit, and in law.

For one thing, this is one country where *bad winners* go on trial. When my Pop surrendered to the Germans in World War II, he was taking his chances. In the end, they fully intended to kill him as a prisoner; they just couldn't get to him at the moment. Which is why he spent five years waiting for the execution that almost happened in the last days of the war. Had he surrendered to the Russians, he might immediately have become one of the thousands of Polish army officers, intellectuals, and other civilians who were summarily shot by the Soviet KGB after they were captured. The Japanese routinely executed both military POWs and civilian detainees during World War II because they considered them less than human and "worthy" of killing.

Our way of dealing with defeated enemies speaks volumes. A prime example of how that works occurred in the latter stages of the war in the Pacific. During some of the heaviest and most brutal fighting of the war, the Japanese military used civilians as shields and forced them to hide grenades on their persons so as to kill as many American soldiers as possible—along with the civilian grenade carriers.

When the fighting stopped, the Japanese civilians and surviving soldiers fully expected to suffer the same fate they had foisted on so many others. Instead, within minutes of the end of fighting, American soldiers were among the civilians, passing out water, chocolates, and hugs to the Japanese children. We fight as hard as anyone, and as brutally in some cases, but we are generally the best sort of winners.

That is not to say that Americans have not violated military, civil, and natural law in wartime. The fact is that, in America, soldiers who do wrong in time of war often end up being prosecuted as the criminals they are. In Vietnam, for example, Lieutenant William Calley was responsible for a massacre of villagers. He was tried, convicted, and sentenced to ten years' imprisonment. More recently, in Iraq, eleven soldiers were charged, convicted, sentenced to military prison, and dishonorably discharged from service in the matter of Abu Ghraib prison. Two others were sentenced to three and ten years in prison and their commander was demoted in rank and officially reprimanded for their actions.

This is not a state of affairs that exists in most nations and is not the way many countries treat their defeated enemies. I can say with historical certainty that the Soviets dealt cruelly with those they defeated. I can be equally sure that in my own Argentina it was never the winning side that ended up in front of the firing squads or inside the prisons.

One way that our basic decency comes through is in the discussion of "illegal internments of enemy combatants." That phrase, as it turns out, is not something recently invented. One of its earliest applications related to Jefferson Davis, the president of the seceding Confederate States of America.

At the end of the Civil War, Davis was arrested and imprisoned. He languished in prison because the assumption on the part of some authorities was that he had to be "guilty" of something. As we are a nation of laws, and those laws are grounded in a common decency, someone began to ask questions. "What, exactly, is the crime of which Mr. Davis is accused?" The answer: There was no crime for which he might be tried. As it turns out, there is nothing in the Constitution specifically referring to the subject of secession. It's one of the few things the Founders failed to provide for. After two years, Davis was let go and not another word of prosecution or trial was ever uttered.

Something similar happened during the Spanish-American War. Unclassified enemy combatants (who had no standing as an official army) were detained by American armed forces. Eventually they were released without further prosecution, largely because of protests and lawsuits initiated back in the States. Although the locales and the players differ, the same dialogue has been renewed since 2001.

CHAPER 10

A Culture of Fresh Starts

In the final scene of the movie *Gone With the Wind*, Scarlett Katie O'Hara, having lost her family, her home, and her South, takes stock of her situation, puts on a brave pout, and utters the classic Americanism: "Tomorrow is another day."

Americans love nothing more than the idea of a fresh start. Our dependable guide to things American, de Tocqueville, wrote, *They take up and leave ten different occupations; they do not fear change as they can enter another activity if the current one does not succeed.*

CHAPTER 11

A Dynamic Sociopolitical Imbalance

MUCH IS MADE IN TODAY'S MEDIA DIALOGUES of the need for Americans to achieve consensus—to find common ground and to desist from obstructionist behavior of every kind. The premise is that others are being difficult or perniciously ignorant when they do not agree with the speaker's own worldview. Apparently, we have forgotten the roots of our political system. *We the People* have come to believe in the fairy tale that America was once the land of universal accord and amiable agreement. More importantly, there are those who believe that, once we have achieved cheerful consensus and are moving in the same direction, things will be delightfully better in this country.

That wasn't the way the Founders saw things—and it is not the way at least half of Americans see our One Nation. Division and dissension were major attendants at the birth of America. Take, for example, the principles behind Madison v. Jefferson—which was not a legal precedent but a political one.

Having rid the country of the despicable George III, James Madison was thoroughly entrenched in the belief that there was nothing wrong with the principle of monarchy—it was only the players who posed the problem. We can sum up his point of view quite simply. Madison believed that there was nothing wrong with autocracy, even perhaps monarchy—presumably, as long as he was to be the monarch in question. James Madison leaned toward the belief that the people should be led…by their betters who would know better on their behalf.

Good thing for us that Thomas Jefferson was around to countervail Madison's view. The interesting thing is that Jefferson was afraid of democracy—at least in total democracy. Much like the Greeks who invented it, Jefferson feared the possibility that democracy could all too easily devolve into mob rule. On the other hand, with the experience of more than twenty years of capricious and pernicious rule under George III fresh in his mind, Jefferson and his adherents had a different solution in mind.

In 1787, the Constitution of the United States enshrined an intentionally divisive form of government—the intent of which is clear for those who read the Letter of Transmittal that accompanied the Constitution to the Continental Congress. The document clearly states,

> *The friends of our country have long seen and desired, that [all power] should be fully and effectually vested in the general government of the Union: But the impropriety of delegating such extensive trust to one body of men is evident—Hence results the necessity of a different organization.*

And *different* it was, by design. Constitutional separation of powers represents a conscious intent to create a positive dynamic of obstructionism and encourage not only differences of opinion, but also a concomitant dissipation of the power of any one aspect of government—a concept to which the British Crown demonstrably did not subscribe at that time.

As it turned out, or perhaps it turned out precisely because of these provisions, no one is unequivocally in charge in America—and that's a stupendous thing! What has happened, historically, is that a particular point of view rises to temporary ascendancy, only to be reversed when the American dynamic imbalance (the naturally centering counterweight of the reactive Americans) is activated at the next election. As long as the pendulum swings slightly right and slightly left, the original intent of the Founders will be preserved, along with our hard-won freedoms, particularly those associated with and supportive of individual liberty and personal initiative.

SECTION II

Markers of the America Code

IN RECENT TIMES, the word "exceptional" when applied to America and American has been burdened by an overload of emotional baggage and political correctitude. This is especially true when referring to "American exceptionalism." To some, the adjective is the badge of a well-earned sense of superiority. To others, it is just another example of national presumptuousness that must be diminished and apologized for.

Whether Americans are better or worse than other people is a question with at least as many answers as the number of people engaged in the discussion. As someone who has made a living understanding and defining the differences among groups of people, I can tell you one thing for sure— Americans are different. Once you take the time to understand and appreciate what brought us to America, how that makes America different from the places we or our ancestors left, and how that combination has created "something else" in a people and a political system, there can be no other conclusion. We are different from those we left behind. In fact, it is those very differences that caused *us*—or our ancestors—to make the journey to America and it is those differences that kept and still keeps *them* over there.

In science and medicine, you may not always be able to understand the underlying condition, but external markers (symptoms) present themselves. When you assemble a sufficient number of these symptoms, you can usually figure out the "disease." The same happens in astronomy, where you may not be able to see a heavenly body but you can clearly view the effect it has on other nearby celestial orbs.

What makes Americans Americans is, at least in part, a matter of genetics. When it comes to congenital Archetypal Americans, you need but look for the genetic "markers." There is decidedly evidence that nations are made up of people who share genetically transmitted markers. For those sensitive to picking up on it, it is often easy to see "the map of Poland" on a Polish person's face—that is because the bulk of Polish people share a common genetic pool, as do the French, the English, the Irish, and so on. Physical characteristics tend to mark individuals as members of national ethnicities. We can't necessarily identify the Polish gene (or genes), but that doesn't make it any less real and present.

When it comes to Archetypal Americans, the genetic markers do not necessarily take the form of physical characteristics. Rather, they tend to define specific actions and values. This is what constitutes the America Code. In the same way that retriever dogs naturally run toward water and expect to come out with something in their mouths, there is something inside prototypical Americans that powers their external actions.

The America Code rests on seven basic observational markers. To understand what makes Americans different, we must understand how these markers define the American character and make it unique.

SEVEN MARKERS OF THE AMERICA CODE

1. We are a national collective of disenfranchised diligent optimists.

2. We are addicted to individual liberty.

3. We flourish through association rather than consensus.

4. We thrive on the principle of possibility.

5. We believe in something greater than ourselves and greater than the state.

6. We wage pragmatic combat in conflicts both national and personal.

7. We are incurably infected by collective congenital amnesia.

CHAPTER 12

Disenfranchised Diligent Optimists

Go anywhere in the world today and say, "I am an American." People will respond in one of two ways. They will be overwhelmingly positive and want to know more about you, tell you stories of their friends and relatives who have visited America, and engage you in talk about American movies, music, books, and politics. Or they will react negatively. They will want to lecture you about American imperialism, tell you how the American system is not as good as their own, and express resentment for the intrusion of American culture into their native values. There is one thing you can be sure of—when people hear the word "America" or "Americans," they are likely to say *very good* or *very bad*. They are very unlikely to say *average* or *just like everybody else*.

For my part, I do not have to ask, "Are Americans different?" I believe that has been amply demonstrated over the past 250 years of our existence. We just don't go about doing what we do like all the other nations on earth. The issue for me, and my purpose in writing this book, is to understand *how Americans are different* from everyone else and how we came to be that way.

Why is it that the words "America" and "Americans" generate so much energy—positive or negative? There is a simple explanation. We didn't end up being different from everyone else on the planet; we started out being different from everyone else on the planet—by design, by purpose, and by our basic constitution, and as a matter of genetics.

The story of America began with what we now call the American Dream. Actually it wasn't so much a dream as it was a vision. The word "dream" implies a temporary state. When you wake from it, you are back in reality. By definition, a dream is something that has only a rare chance of realization. "Vision," on the other hand, implies an intention, a goal, a purpose—and has at least a 50 percent chance of being achieved. Visions drive actions. Those actions change realities.

From the very beginning, the American Vision has been startlingly simple—a fresh start in a new place where the rules are different than they were back home, rules that don't capriciously prevent me from being the best me I can be. As Washington Irving once said, "Great minds have purposes; others have wishes." America is a land built on purposes—millions and millions of them.

We are a land of immigrants. We are a nation of nations. It has been that way from the very beginning. Alexis de Tocqueville noticed the difference immediately upon arriving in this country in the 1830s. On his first sight of this new America, de Tocqueville wrote to a friend at home:

> *Imagine, my dear friend, if you can a society formed of all nations of the world…people having different languages, beliefs, opinions: In a*

word, a society without roots, without memories, without prejudices,
without routines, without common ideas, without a national character,
yet a hundred times happier than our own.

Many nations, yes. But remarkably similar in a number of key ways. Whether English, or Spanish, or Polish, or Portuguese—we Americans have some things in common that make us more American than English, Spanish, Polish, or Portuguese.

Is it even remotely reasonable to assume that the people who came to America at great expense, great risk, and against tremendous odds could possibly be exactly the same as the people they left behind? When you consider what it takes to become an immigrant—what it takes to leave behind everything you know, everything you have, and in some ways everything you are, to cross an ocean and start your life again—you have to consider the possibility that immigrants are a particular kind of people and that those who make the journey are fundamentally unlike the ones who stay behind.

I have more than a little insight into what it takes to be an immigrant. After World War II, my mother and father traveled to four different countries on three different continents before finally making it to America. Their goal was always America, but the four legs of the journey took them more than ten years. Yet they never hesitated to continue trying for the goal in a kind of spawning salmon drive toward some new, unfamiliar, yet simultaneously comfortable destination.

In spite of tremendous obstacles, they first traveled to Italy, then to England, then to Argentina, and finally to America. Their story is not unusual among the tens of millions of immigrants who came to this country. At every stage of their journey, they kept believing in their heart of hearts that there was something special about America—no, they didn't just believe, they knew it was the place where they belonged.

Because of my immigrant heritage and because I make my living trying to understand why people do what they do and what motivates them to specific action, I became nearly obsessed with trying to understand what it is that drives people to become Americans. I think the answer is quite literally a matter of genetic disposition. By their very makeup, Americans are not only capable of withstanding the demands of emigration and immigration, but also driven to bold actions by a specific set of predilections that are part of their biological nature. People who come to America as immigrants are inclined by their very nature to do so.

So it naturally follows that people who come to America are not representative of all the people from the places they leave behind. They are, in fact, a unique slice of their nation's population. For the most part, people who come to America do so because the circumstances in which they find themselves back home have become intolerable to them. The price of staying and enduring becomes higher than the cost of leaving.

Those who take action have a fundamentally different makeup from those who do not. Those who come to American as immigrants are by nature *disenfranchised diligent optimists*. They are *disenfranchised* in the sense that they do not fit in with the operational plan, the natural order of things, back home. Whatever they want to do, who they want to be, is decided or diminished by the system and by their "betters."

It is my view (based on historical analysis, personal observations, and extensive conversations with knowledgeable people on both sides of the Atlantic) that in Europe, in the past and to a large extent even today, who you are is ultimately dictated by who your parents were and what your history is. The European mind-set is that each person is given a proper place in society and is expected to make the most of that place—but not to insist on aspiring to more. In America, you make your own place and only suffer the limits that you yourself create. Being disenfranchised only makes you uncomfortable. To get from there to here you need to take action, to do something, to make a diligent effort at changing your status and your circumstances. The diligent disenfranchised make a plan, make a move, and make a change.

But starting on the journey to America is only the beginning of the test. For most immigrants, the road here typically had many twists, turns, bumps, obstacles, and trials—more than enough to wear down the timid. Judging by my own family's odyssey, the only thing you can count on to help you through is optimism—the belief that no matter how dark the moment, the ultimate result is not only worth the suffering, but is absolutely achievable. This higher-level optimism is not teachable or learnable—it is natural to few and alien to many.

History shows us that the immigrants' optimistic belief and vision are tested often. In the end, only those who continue to be optimistic throughout their struggle make the journey successfully. The people who came to America originally, who are coming to America today, and who will continue to come to America and to continue to define it, are by definition disenfranchised, diligent, and preponderantly optimistic.

I believe this is something that operates at a genetic level. While there may not be an electron microscope powerful enough to see it, nor a chemical analysis sophisticated enough to test it, there exists some gene sequence that is carried by everyone who is a disenfranchised diligent optimist. The same is true for most of their children.

You may think that I'm overstating the idea of a genetic basis for the American character. But take a moment to think about the way the world really works. I have a friend who has a Bernese mountain dog (officially the Berner Sennenhund). The breed was developed in the Alps around Bern, Switzerland, for the singular and specific purpose of rescuing people in deep snow in high places.

The particular dog I know lives in Connecticut and has never seen Alpine snow, has never been anywhere near the Alps, and the only thing she has ever rescued is a piece of steak from an unattended plate. Nonetheless, the animal's predisposition at some genetic level makes her incredibly happy to cavort in the deepest snow, at least the deepest snow possible in New England. What's even more incredible is that, having been bred to work on hillsides and the particularly steep slopes of high mountains, Bernese mountain dogs take exceptional delight in standing at an angle—as if leaning on a slope in some high Swiss valley.

When you apply the same kind of observations to some of the great families of America, or of the world for that matter, there also appears to be a connection between genetics and traits such as leadership, industriousness, and perhaps even a "success" gene.

Many members of some of these families even have the look of leadership about them. This is no accident—it is a matter of intentional genetics and selective breeding. A majority of the Kennedys, the Roosevelts, and the Rockefellers just *look* like they're important—the biological peers of royals across the sea. Other families may not look the part physically but tend to have a propensity to success that is demonstrably higher than that of the average citizenry; more members of such families enjoy success and naturally traffic in initiative than most other families.

I doubt that we could successfully map the genome sequence that specifically orients the Bernese mountain dog to do what it does, to be what it is, and to enjoy what it enjoys. Nonetheless, the observational evidence is there to be noted. Most of us are more familiar with a more common breed of working dog known as Labrador retrievers. Here again we don't understand exactly why, and we can't exactly map the genetics, but put a Labrador retriever near any water, and she will jump in and fetch back anything that you throw—Labs just can't help themselves.

Wherever we came from, we came to America because we intuitively appreciated that we would never fit in the system we left behind. We knew that there was a "they" who would not allow us to be ourselves or to do what we felt was best for ourselves. Giving orders came naturally to those in charge and taking orders was equally not the natural order of our immigrant predecessors. Nor is it the nature of today's immigrants.

Don't get me wrong; there are diligent people all over the globe. There are optimistic people in all countries and on all continents. But there are different types of diligent optimists—three distinct types, in fact. Disenfranchised diligent optimists are the ones who make a new life somewhere else. They are the natural-born emigrants, many of whom have headed our way from the very discovery of the New World.

There are also *compliant diligent optimists*—those who fit into the scheme of things and work within their heritage systems. There are also the adaptive *lemonade makers,* who tend to make excellent lemonade from the bitterest or sourest of circumstances. These we might call *adaptive diligent optimists.* They accept that they have no control and do not hold the whip hand, and go on from there to make the absolute most of their circumstances.

I think it important to talk about the two diligent optimist types that are a contrast to the disenfranchised diligent optimists who I believe are the defining cultural American archetype because not everyone came to America by choice and some got here a lot sooner than the American Vision.

The latter groups would include African-Americans and Native Americans, among whom there are decidedly many diligent optimists, people of hope, and people who focus on achievement and making things better. Historically, neither group was given the opportunity to choose to come to America or join the American Vision because America was either thrust upon them or descended upon them against their will.

It doesn't take much to see excellent examples of diligent optimists among African-Americans and Native Americans; both groups made very positive and important contributions to American history, American progress, and the America that we know and love. Ironically, these groups were disenfranchised by some of the same people who came to America specifically because they themselves were disenfranchised back home. It is reasonable to assume that, given the same opportunity, many African-Americans may well have chosen to immigrate here on their own. Native Americans certainly carry the disenfranchised diligent optimist gene in one form or another as they did choose to make the journey long before there was a political entity called America.

So, if America is largely a land of immigrants, and immigrants are disenfranchised diligent optimists from around the globe, where do these foundational American people come from? What national makeups, and what national characters, have had the strongest influence on creating America and Americans?

America is one country with no single national majority. We are a nation of nations on the one hand and we are a nation of minorities on the other hand. According to the 2010 Bureau of the Census only 7.2 percent of Americans surveyed identified themselves as being of "American" origin, which means that more than 92 percent of Americans are connected enough to their original national backgrounds to still identify with them. In only four states (Arkansas, Kentucky, Tennessee, and West Virginia) did a plurality of census respondents identify themselves as Americans. That would make these the only truly American states.

According to the most recently available information from US government sources, the single largest national group in the United States of America is German—at more than 15 percent or about 43 million. This fact might surprise some readers. Even more fascinating—there are more than half as many German-Americans as there are Germans in Germany, which has a population of roughly 82 million. Interestingly enough, Benjamin Franklin, as early as in the 1750s was concerned that America would become a German nation. Well, we didn't, but there are more German-Americans than any other American subgroup.

Following the Germans, the Irish make up the next largest national group at about 11 percent of the country's population. This is one group that effectively reversed the balance of mother country to colony. There are at this moment some 30 million Irish-Americans—which is about six times as many Irish as there are in Ireland.

The third-largest national origin group in America is those people who identify themselves as English—roughly 8 percent or about 25 million Americans.

Americans who consider themselves to be of American origin are the fourth-largest national group and a mere 7.2 percent or about 20 million people (out of more than 330 million). The next largest group is Mexicans, who make up roughly 6.5 percent or 18 million Americans, followed closely by Italian-Americans, who make up about 5.6 percent or 16 million Americans.

The next two groups are the Polish and the French with roughly 3.2 percent or about 9 million Americans each. The Scots and the Dutch at almost 2 percent each are the last of the groups to fall above a full percentage point. Each of the other nationalities that make up America accounts for less than 1 percent, and in most cases much less than 1 percent, of the American national composition.

Some of you may have noticed, and may actually wish to call to my attention, the apparently glaring omission of any mention of African-Americans or Native Americans, who make up substantial portions of the American populace. After all, African-Americans number roughly 12.3 percent or over 40 million Americans, and Native Americans add up to just under 1 percent, or roughly 3 million people. Moreover, in the previous paragraphs I have absolutely failed to mention Hispanic-Americans, or Latinos.

This is not an accident nor is it an omission. In order to make the entire concept of this book meaningful and in particular the conversation about national personalities as they relate to the America Code, we have to be able to identify the specific national characters involved.

There is no nation of Africa—any more than there is a nationality of "Europeans," "Asians," or "Hispanics." In fact, historically, there have been many different, distinct nationalities on the continent of Africa. We don't precisely know to which national groups most African-Americans belong. As to "Hispanic-Americans," I, as a born Argentine, am acutely aware that Argentines do not consider themselves to have much in common with Brazilians, any more than Peruvians feel close to Uruguayans. Each Latin American nation is distinct from its neighbors and similarly different from Spain. The fact is that the vast majority of Latinos or Hispanic-Americans are identifiable as Mexicans and I've included them in the list above as such.

In the same vein, in the context of this book, we can't talk about Native Americans as a category without considering the differences between the many Indian nations. Can we say that the Iroquois national character is exactly the same as that of the Aztec or that Comanches and Seminoles are more alike than they are different?

In truth, when we talk about the formative national characters of America, we really have to go back to the foundational nations that contributed to what we have ended up being in a significant way. Those are mainly Germans, English, Irish, and to some smaller extent Dutch and Scots. All are generally considered to be diligent people with a strong sense of right and wrong and a demonstrated desire for "something better beyond the horizon" throughout their respective histories.

More importantly, it is in particular the disenfranchised diligent optimists of those nations that laid the foundation for what America is today. The subsequent waves of immigrants have a fundamental connection and an affinity to the values of these first foundational people because they too are disenfranchised diligent optimists first and foremost.

It is as if you could visualize taking a block of disenfranchised diligent optimists out of Germany and dropping them in America. Then going back and picking up a disenfranchised diligent optimists block from England. Then continue doing the same for Ireland, Italy, Poland, and so on, and so on, and so on.

The net result is that we wind up with a country that has a higher density of disenfranchised diligent optimists than any other nation anywhere on earth. That is precisely the core of the genetic predisposition that makes America America and Americans Americans.

CHAPTER 13

Addicted to Individual Liberty

DEEPLY INGRAINED IN THE AMERICA CODE is some gene sequence that predisposes its carriers to the pursuit of individual liberty on a nearly pathological scale. Americans don't just value personal liberty—we are virtually addicted to it; without it we suffer, shrivel, and die.

This aspect of the code has roots in some of the nationalities that contributed to the foundational makeup of the American nation and continue to pass it on from generation to generation. It was a tradition among Viking warriors that they would willingly die in battle, particularly if there were promises of enriching booty for the victors. But Viking warriors fought with their chieftains, not for them, and decidedly not under them. Traditionally, the Viking warrior bent a knee to no man. English blood runs thick with Viking genes. Among the most dreaded of Germanic tribes were the Saxons, who served as effective mercenaries for anyone willing to pay a fee or a ransom. The Saxons, too, had a strong bent toward enterprise (often larcenous) and individual freedom. Between rape, pillaging, and settlement, these two tribes heavily influenced the character of what is now Great Britain.

Another group of noteworthy individualists, the Celts, were the familial progenitors of the Irish, many of whom left the Emerald Isle rather than continue to suffer humiliations and subjugations at the hands of the English. They kept up the fight for their own voice and freedoms from the first English occupation of Ireland in the 1600s right up until the final peace accords as recently as 2007.

Poles (who make up the seventh-largest national ethnicity in America) have been historically individualistic to the extreme. For nearly 140 years

(1652 to 1791), any individual member of the Polish Parliament could undo not only the act under consideration, but the entire session of the legislature by merely standing up in the hall and proclaiming "I object!" Luckily that extreme of individualism eventually went the way of the dodo—which was about as smart as the notion of the "*liberum* veto" itself (loosely translated from the Latin, the phrase means "I do not allow!"—or more colloquially, "I object!").

So, if the first marker of the America Code, being a disenfranchised diligent optimist, is what impels you to make the journey in the first place, then being genetically coded for individual liberty is what gives you that intense belief in your own abilities that sustains you through trials, tribulations, and obstacles in getting to the better place of your own making.

Contrary to some popular thinking, America is not built around the notion of the common good, and certainly not around the notion of sacrificing the individual for that common good. Americans believe that kind of thinking is what created Soviet socialism, propels Chinese communism, and generally powers or powered, in its most extreme forms, most totalitarian regimes—including the monarchy of George III.

The prototypical American believes that the highest good is the achievement of his or her own personal goals—not that Americans don't know how to work together or believe in the value of working together. But we will explore how that concept plays out in the America Code a little bit later on.

At the simple human level, the drive to individual liberty is about being able to achieve two simple goals. The first is the right to carve out a space all your own, a place that you define and over which you have fundamental control. The second is the ability to decide what you want to do, when you want to do it, and why you want to do it. We see this idea powerfully expressed in American literature, and in particular the literature of the American West. In this genre there are many references to animals running wild, running free, untethered and unbroken.

The individual spirit, unbroken, unfettered, and uncompromised, is an immensely popular theme for Americans because it reaches to the very essence of who we are. That is why Americans have such empathy for the mustang, the wild horse of the expansive American prairie.

America is a democracy, but a democracy of a different color. While the word "democracy" itself means "rule of the people" in the original Greek, the actual form of government practiced in ancient Greece was anything but democratic. It was democracy of the elite, by the elite, and for the elite. The freedoms referred to were reserved specifically for those people who were part of the ruling class. In fact, the very idea of democracy as we understand it, where every person gets a vote and has the right to participate in national decision-making, frightened the devil out of the Greeks.

In the original Greek model of democracy to which we so often refer, the assumption was that a group of elite people who knew better than the common rabble would act in the best interests of everyone else and should make the serious decisions affecting the nation. As we will see later in this book, there are still forces in the America who prefer this interpretation of the concept of democracy.

In the same way, centuries later, when the English lords forced King John to sign the Magna Carta, the freedoms guaranteed in that document applied to the nobility alone. That is essentially the circumstance in which the first Americans found themselves. Meaningful national decision-making was meant to be the sole province of those who were thought to be better than the rest of us and, therefore, naturally presumed to be better equipped to make the *right* decisions on our behalf.

The difference between our form of democracy and the original proposition is that we Americans assume that everyone is *special* and in that capacity has an equal right to make decisions for themselves. In fact, it is only by founding a nation on the premise of individual liberty that we could hope to pull together the inveterate disenfranchised diligent optimists who settled this continent into a meaningful political entity.

Even though they were clearly among the ruling class, the Founders had an intrinsic sense that individual liberty was the fundamental operating principle of the universe—and that, at least in America, the premise would become the practice. No surprise then that the phrase "endowed by their Creator with certain inalienable rights...among these are life, liberty, and the pursuit of happiness" made its way to the foundational documents that created the political system on which this country is based.

The fact is that long before the Declaration of Independence and the

Constitution enshrined the idea of individual liberty, it was already a fundamental operating premise of the America Code that had brought natural Americans here and represented a kind of natural working order for American relationships. The assumption that I could do my own thing, but choose to participate in the business of the nation is an exceptionally empowering idea for citizens anywhere. It also defines the American understanding of the proper relationship between the individual and the government at every level. That relationship here is different from other places on the planet because it is essentially a relationship of equals.

The principles, protections, and laws under which we operate as a country were the result of the fundamental nature of a people who believed that individual liberty is the paramount concern and should be the paramount freedom for every human being. If we need to work together, goes the American mantra, then at least I get to choose where and how I will participate in that endeavor.

A perfect example of how Americans value individual liberty comes from what is known as the Gadsden Flag. In 1775, when the United States Navy was established, Congress authorized the mustering of five companies of marines to accompany the navy on its missions. The first marines carried yellow painted drums that depicted a coiled rattlesnake with thirteen rattles and the motto "Don't tread on me." Clearly the rattlesnake logo was intended to represent the thirteen colonies admonishing the British Empire not to step on their new freedoms. At the same time, it is a perfect expression of how Americans feel about their individual liberties.

CHAPTER 14

Association, Yea. Consensus, Not So Much

BASED ON THE THIRD MARKER OF THE AMERICA CODE, our national motto might well be "If there is something worth doing, it only needs one American to get things started."

Our old friend Alexis de Tocqueville said it very well in the 1840s:

When a private individual mediates an undertaking, however directly connected it may be to the welfare of society, he never thinks of soliciting the cooperation of the government, but he publishes his plan, offers to execute it himself, courts the assistance of other individuals, and struggles manfully against all obstacles. Undoubtedly he is often less successful than the state might have been in his position, but in the end the sum of these private undertakings far exceeds what the government could have done.

Something about Americans' fundamental internal makeup makes it possible for us to subscribe to the notion that there is a greater whole and that we are required somehow to participate in and to subject ourselves to that greater whole only when and only insofar as necessary. On the other hand, once we appreciate that there is something that needs to be done and that we might need the help of others, we reach out to those others—and they to us. We then connect ourselves to them in some kind of relatively loose and flexible association so that whatever it is that we want to undertake can be undertaken. When that project is finished, we go back to our own individual tracks.

Throughout history and even to this day in Europe and other parts of the world, the natural order of things is that a citizen who sees the need for something to be done immediately petitions the government to make things happen. Government takes on the project and enlarges its mandate in the process.

As de Tocqueville observed, and this time I won't quote him directly but rather paraphrase—if something happens in the street, the natural tendency of Americans is not to call for the appropriate officials but to immediately gather as a group to fix the problem. After the problem is fixed, the group breaks up and the members go their own way.

Creating a company, creating a government, or creating an entirely new national system of doing things, for Americans, is no more than a call for working together for the moment. Whether it is because we firmly believe that we can figure things out for ourselves—a key trait of disenfranchised diligent optimists that certainly validates the extreme individualism and inventiveness that we possess—or whether it is because we are suspicious of the ultimate cost of any help offered, we Americans firmly believe that if it's worth doing, it is worth doing by ourselves first and foremost. We have been and will continue to be an innovative people. Innovation usually takes place in one mind and then infects others.

Innovative is pretty much what you have to be to show up in a place where there is nothing, then figure out what you need to do, and finally decide what you need to get it done. Most of the time you need to do things for yourself or by reaching out to those who are most readily accessible, most willing, and most likely to offer their direct help as they might need yours some day. One of the reasons Americans have a reputation for being uncooperative and uncompliant and unwilling to wait for instructions is that throughout much of our personal familial and national history, waiting to be led would have served to get us killed or enslaved instead.

During what was known as the starving time in Jamestown colony, nearly 80 percent of the settlers died. More than 70 percent of the women who settled Plymouth colony in Massachusetts died shortly after arrival. Their men did a little better with a 58 percent death rate. Those who remained in America were the hardiest of survivors. As a nation of natural-born survivors, we tend to assume that we know everything and have all the answers—at least all the answers that we need to solve the problems in front of us. This is something pretty normal for a group of people who have had to invent a great many things from scratch, starting, of course, with the idea of a republic built around individual liberty.

We tend to believe in collective action rather than common action. The difference between the two is that in collective activity, you do what needs to be done but stay separate from the group in which you are participating at the moment. In common activity, you work together because you share some common, unifying tie with the others. As Americans, we tend to be action-oriented and that means we tend to be task-oriented.

Ultimately this enterprise of ones (collective and yet singular) sets the stage for what we will later discuss as the central operating principle of America from the very beginning and on into the future—the notion of individual initiative.

CHAPTER 15

Obsessed with Possibility

DEEP IN THE CODE FOR AMERICA is an expectation of possibility rather than entitlement. This country is not grounded in what you can expect the government to give you. It is based on what you can expect the government to do to stay out of your way while you go about achieving the possibilities that are your inalienable right to pursue.

In the course of his presidential campaign in 1968, Robert F. Kennedy perfectly articulated the fourth marker of the American Code when he said, "There are those that look at things the way they are, and ask why? I dream of things that never were, and ask why not?" Americans subscribe to the principle of possibility in a big way.

There are stories (whether they are true or not, they are perfectly American in nature) that Bill Lear, the inventor of the small, personal class of jet planes that became known as Lear Jets, was told by aeronautical engineers at the time that his jet was incapable of flying. Apparently Mr. Lear had not studied enough aeronautics to know that his jet was impractical. Luckily for us and for aeronautics as a whole, he continued to believe in the idea that a small jet could be successful. Mr. Lear focused more on the possibility that it could fly than on the probability espoused by others that it could not. How very American of Mr. Lear!

Possibility fuels invention. America is acknowledged to be a nation of inventors. Some say, Mark Twain among them, that if all we had ever invented was a country where people could be free, that accomplishment alone would be enough to keep us at the top of the invention ladder for centuries to come. As Americans, we are driven by what might be, what could be, what can possibly be, much more than we are propelled by what is or what must be. Considering that we came from circumstances where limits were continually imposed, it is only reasonable to conclude that the people who left countries with such restrictions would be the ones least able to tolerate such strictures.

We Americans are all for the status quo as long as that status quo allows room for the change we desire. In our American mind-set, change is the status quo—particularly because it allows room for us to consider the possibilities that would best meet our desires and intentions. Otherwise we would spend most of our lives adapting to realities that other people create rather than inventing the possibilities within which we get to do what we want to do.

If we operated on the principle of *probability* rather than *possibility*, there probably would never have been an America. Take, for example, the case of Christopher Columbus and compare the way we think today to how people thought then. Any well-executed professional feasibility study of his proposed voyage would have concluded that "nothing will be found, you will all die, and there will be no success whatsoever." Fortunately for us, men like Columbus and Amerigo Vespucci and Giovanni da Verrazano and all of the other explorers and settlers didn't come to America because they were assured of success. Quite the contrary: certainty, as far as they could measure it, was on the side of failure. Even these early explorers, operating on the possibility principle, were also operating in a way consistent with the America Code.

It is sobering to realize how high the odds against success were in the early days of this country—in other words, the probability versus the possibility. Something on the order of 60 to 80 percent of the initial colonists who settled in what is now America died. An incredibly high number of the Jamestown settlers never made it. That was not the only colony where the reality was far more failure than success. The Roanoke Colony disappeared without a trace. You didn't come to America with chance in your favor.

Throughout the history of America the people who have defined the country have done so not because they were guaranteed a positive result, but because they believed in the possible validity of their efforts and the chance they might be right. They were dedicated to the possibility that things could be better than they were back home. If they had operated on the principle of certainty instead, they would have stayed home and found a way to live with the devil they knew.

We believe that when people act believing that something is possible it often becomes possible and that if enough of us believe in something strongly enough and really work at it, it becomes not only possible but inevitable.

CHAPTER 16

Belief in Something Greater Than Ourselves — But Not the State

THE ORIGINAL THINKING OF THE FOUNDERS was that the power of government should not be in the hands of the church and the power of the church should not be in the hands of the government. They had seen and felt firsthand the consequences of a national church headed by the same officials who made the laws of the land. Technically, this is still the state of affairs with the Anglican Church today.

According to the official website of the Anglican Church,[4]

> *The Sovereign holds the title 'Defender of the Faith and Supreme Governor of the Church of England'.... Archbishops and bishops are appointed by The Queen on the advice of the Prime Minister, who considers the names selected by a Church Commission. They take an oath of allegiance to The Queen on appointment and may not resign without Royal authority.*

> *The connection between Church and State is also symbolised by the fact that the 'Lords Spiritual' (consisting of the Archbishops of Canterbury and York and 24 diocesan bishops) sit in the House of Lords. Parish priests also take an oath of allegiance to The Queen....*

> *Since 1919, the Synod (formerly called the Church Assembly) has had the power to pass Measures on any matter concerning the Church of England. Following acceptance of the Measures by both Houses of Parliament (which cannot amend them), they are submitted for Royal Assent and become law.*

All of which means that the religion, the head of state, the legislature, and the clergy are pretty much interchangeable when it comes to a particular, sanctioned, singular religion of the country. It is precisely this state of affairs that the Founders wanted to avoid because many of them had gone through the worst of the abuses such a church/state connection makes possible.

They were looking for a godly nation where people could worship according to their conscience—or not—and face no legal sanctions or penalties for doing so. What they were not looking for was a godless nation from which religion was legislatively or judicially excluded. Other than the idea of a single state-sanctioned official religion, Americans have always been, and apparently still are, okay with God in the national picture.

Alexis de Tocqueville, the French examiner of the American experience, had mostly good things to say on the value of combining God with an independent nation:

> *Religion in America takes no direct part in the government of society, but it must be regarded as the first of their political institutions... I do not know whether all Americans have a sincere faith in their religion—for who can search the human heart?—but I am certain that they hold it to be indispensable to the maintenance of republican institutions. This opinion is not peculiar to a class of citizens or to a party, but it belongs to the whole nation and to every rank of society.*

And...

> *Moreover, almost all the sects of the United States are comprised within the great unity of Christianity, and Christian morality is everywhere the same. In the United States the sovereign authority is religious, and consequently hypocrisy must be common; but there is no country in the whole world in which the Christian religion retains a greater influence over the souls of men than in America, and there can be no greater proof of its utility, and of its conformity to human nature, than that its influence is most powerfully felt over the most enlightened and free nation of the earth.*

> *The Americans combine the notions of Christianity and of liberty so intimately in their minds, that it is impossible to make them conceive the one without the other; and with them this conviction does not spring from that barren traditional faith which seems to vegetate in the soul rather than to live.*

There are certain populations in Europe whose unbelief is only equaled by their ignorance and their debasement, while in America one of the freest and most enlightened nations in the world fulfills all the outward duties of religion with fervor.

Upon my arrival in the United States, the religious aspect of the country was the first thing that struck my attention; and the longer I stayed there, the more did I perceive the great political consequences resulting from this state of things, to which I was unaccustomed. In France I had almost always seen the spirit of religion and the spirit of freedom pursuing courses diametrically opposed to each other; but in America I found that they were intimately united, and that they reigned in common over the same country.

Some might assume that a belief in a higher power is not the universal it was back in the 1800s. But they would be wrong. God is still important to a preponderant majority of Americans, according to a Gallup survey taken in May 2011. Surprisingly, although not all Americans believe to the same degree, more Americans find consensus on this account than on many other national issues (see **Table 16-1**).

And according to a 2002 Pew Research Study,

Religion is much more important to Americans than to people living in other wealthy nations. Six-in-ten (59 percent) people in the U.S. say religion plays a very important role in their lives. This is roughly twice the percentage of self-avowed religious people in Canada (30 percent), and an even higher proportion when compared with Japan and Western Europe. Americans' views are closer to people in developing nations than to the publics of developed nations.

If current immigration trends continue and Latin-Americans grow as a percentage of the US population, Pew's next survey is likely to show an even higher percentage of Americans who say religion is important in their lives. The forty-four-nation survey of the Pew Global Attitudes Project shows stark global regional divides over the personal importance of religion. In Africa, no fewer than eight in ten people in any country see religion as very important personally. Majorities in every Latin American country also subscribe to that view.[5]

Table 16-1. Belief in God			
Belief in God	Percentage	Belief in God	Percentage
National adults	92	East	86
		South	96
Men	90	Midwest	91
Women	94	West	92
18–29	84	Conservatives	98
30–49	94	Moderates	91
59–64	94	Liberals	85
65+	94		
		Republicans	98
High school or less	92	Independents	89
Some college	93	Democrats	90
College grad	94		
Postgraduate education	87		

Gallup Poll, May 2011

CHAPTER 17

Pragmatic Combatants

IN 1968, THE UNITED STATES OF AMERICA WAS DEEPLY EMBROILED in a drawn-out conflict in Vietnam in an effort to stop the expansion of communism in Asia—an effort at which the French had failed in 1954. In January 1968, tens of thousands of Vietcong insurgents attacked hundreds of hamlets and the major cities of Vietnam, including Saigon and Hue. After bloody fighting throughout much of the country, most of the Vietcong were killed or captured and the offensive was stopped cold.

By May the North Vietnamese and the United States agreed to meet in Paris in order to begin negotiations toward peace. Based on the fact that most of the attacks by the Vietcong and the North Vietnamese army had been repulsed and so many of the Vietcong had been eliminated, the Tet offensive was clearly a military victory for the United States. So why were we negotiating with the enemy just a few months later?

In his book *A Vietcong Memoir: An Inside Account of the Vietnam War and Its Aftermath*, Truong Nhu Tang, one of the founders of the Vietcong, writes that he could not believe what happened after the Tet offensive. As he and the other leaders of that organization saw it, the United States had won a decisive military victory on the battlefield, inflicting massive defeats and setbacks on both the Vietcong and the North Vietnamese army, who had failed to precipitate the popular revolt of the South Vietnamese people that the attack was meant to incite.

Instead of the United States claiming victory and consolidating its gains, what Tang and his colleagues witnessed was a success publicly presented as a massive failure in the American press and accepted as such by the American people. They could not believe their eyes when American public opinion, and an apparent loss of the will to fight, handed them victory in place of defeat. It was unfortunate for Tang that this was also the moment when his North Vietnamese "partners" finally showed their hand as invaders rather than friends, although by this point, the Vietcong had ceased to be a viable fighting force thanks to the efforts of American troops during Tet. In the end, the Vietcong were sold out by their partners and South Vietnam ceased to exist.

In 1973, as part of the Paris Peace Accords, the United States pulled out of Vietnam, setting the stage for what ended up as the full-fledged invasion and elimination of the Republic of South Vietnam—a clear victory for Russian-backed communism in Southeast Asia—although America's presence in Vietnam did forestall the expansion of the communist doctrine to much of the rest of the region.

In a sense, the Vietnam War was not only a gut-wrenching national tragedy for America, but also an excellent illustration of how we Americans go about getting into and out of conflicts. If you ever plan to go to war with America, it would serve you well to understand the process that Americans apply not just to combat, but to conflicts personal, national, and political. As humorist Will Rogers once observed, *America has never lost a war or won a conference.*

The sixth marker of the America Code tells us that the citizens of the United States of America are reluctant to fight, implacable in combat, first to take a time-out, and first to forgive. In short, we are totally pragmatic combatants.

We Americans take our time getting into a struggle. We continually weigh the necessity versus the cost of the fight. Inertia favors our remaining out of the battle. We are slow to anger. It is not that we are afraid of getting into a fight: history shows that we are perfectly capable of handling ourselves once we do. It's just that we don't want to fight until we feel it's absolutely, inescapably necessary.

Much press has been given to what journalist Tom Brokaw calls America's "Greatest Generation," willing warriors dedicated to fighting for the highest ideals in World War II. The truth is that even after Pearl Harbor fully a quarter of American citizens continued to opt for sitting it out. Throughout the war, questions continued to be raised by many people about whether it was a good idea to be in that fight at all.

Japan's Admiral Yamamoto, the architect of the attack on Pearl Harbor, had gone to school in the United States. He understood better than other Japanese planners that America would not react immediately even if it had the resources to do so. As he saw it, there would be a six-month window during which Japan needed to make as many advances as possible. At the end of that time, the best the Japanese Empire could hope for would be a negotiated resolution.

As it turned out, the timing was right. It was the opening gambit that was wrong and ultimately proved catastrophic for the Japanese. At the start of the Second World War, the Japanese assumption was that destroying the US naval forces at Pearl Harbor would be a necessary prerequisite for seizing territory throughout the Pacific. Unfortunately for the Japanese, the date that will live in infamy (December 7, 1941) turned out to be a small military victory and a powerful rallying cry for America.

It was in fact exactly the kind of event that Americans require to move from inactivity to forceful and focused action. The attack on Pearl Harbor was a crisis and Americans love nothing better than rallying around a crisis. In a crisis, we pull together and we fight! As Americans, we need something around which to organize and leverage the best of our energies and skills because our natural predisposition is not to work together until and unless there is a cause that gives us no alternative.

The more daunting the task, the more we relish taking it on, as President Kennedy once observed:

Why choose [going to the moon] as our goal?...[You] may well ask why climb the highest mountain? Why, 35 years ago, fly the Atlantic?...

We choose to go to the moon. We choose to go to the moon in this decade and do the other things, not because they are easy, but because they are hard, because that goal will serve to organize and measure the best of our energies and skills, because that challenge is one that we are willing to accept, one we are unwilling to postpone, and one which we intend to win, and the others, too.

Perhaps this is a simple extension of the Minuteman ideal. We dote on the vision of citizen soldiers taking their guns down from above the mantelpiece and going off to respond to a heinous attack on one and all—whether the attackers are the Indians, the French, the British, or the communists.

Once engaged, America is not the kind of enemy you want to make. We may be slow to anger, but we are capable of developing a short fuse rapidly. Perhaps it is precisely because we are slow to anger that once the punching actually starts we tend to throw many and hard blows. Moreover, because America is such a resource-rich place and because we are an inventive people, we are prepared and able to do anything necessary to win the scrapes we get into.

In a very real sense, we became a country against the greatest odds because at a time of crisis we knew how to pool our resources and tackle even the deadliest of challenges. For as long as the mission is right and achievable, most of us will favor continuing the fight. And that is the key—to put our hearts, our souls, and our lives on the line, we need to understand the reason for the battle. More importantly, we need to believe in that reason and believe in the mission. Americans prefer a "good" crisis with a definable beginning, a middle, and a clearly foreseeable end over an protracted struggle with no perceivable end in sight. Once our beliefs and that sense of mission wane, our left brains take over quite quickly. We intuitively make the cost-benefit analysis. We are incited to get into combat.

We rationalize our way out of it.

This is one of the reasons other nations often miscalculate what they see as our national lack of focus, will, and purpose. Being American, with such a dynamic streak of built-in individuality and a desire to go our own way, we find it impossible to maintain a sense of collective commitment for very long. This is the very reason why we are always interested in decisive victories and why we always dread extended conflicts.

We respond naturally and with full commitment to a crisis—ready to go in a minute. We also respond naturally to the end of a crisis—ready to pack up and leave in a minute after the crisis is resolved—or at least until we begin to see it as either resolvable or beyond a continued investment.

That is what happened in Vietnam. Partly because of the Tet offensive and partly because we had come to believe either that the war was unwinnable or that the cost to our culture and our society made it undesirable to go on, we basically called a halt. As a people, and as a nation, there are no sweeter words for Americans to hear than "mission accomplished."

By 1987 the first contingent of American tourists returned to Ho Chi Minh City. In 2010, US imports from Vietnam totaled some $15 billion. We also exported nearly $4 billion to Vietnam.

CHAPTER 18

Collective Congenital Amnesiacs

THE SEVENTH MARKER OF THE AMERICA CODE embraces the understanding that no people on the face of the planet have shorter memories than Americans. After the Soviet Union collapsed, what happened in Bosnia and Herzegovina and other places in that part of the world was very difficult for Americans to understand. Most of us could not even begin to understand how people could go from apparently peaceful coexistence as fellow countrymen to committing atrocities against each other in such a very short period of time. Not to mention that they were demanding to form separate nations—and we thought they were separate nations already.

The fact is, the people of the Balkans are more like the rest of the world than they are like Americans. They have unresolved issues going back hundreds of years that still fester and drive people to unimaginable actions in the present. These hatreds and animosities go back well before the Soviet army arrived after the Second World War, well before the Austro-Hungarian Empire made its mark on the area, and back to the times when the Turks held sway in the region. What Americans saw and what we could not understand arose from the simple fact that there was a 400-year time-out imposed by the invading armies on a fundamental disagreement between Balkan Muslims and Christians. The instant the imperial referees left the stadium, not only did the contest resume, but it did so with the total intensity it would have had 400 years earlier. No hurt and no grievance had been forgotten or forgiven over the four ensuing centuries.

Harboring grudges for that long, or even a fraction of that time, is not something that Americans are naturally inclined to do or even to understand. Part of being the children of a particular brand of immigrants means that we are coded for collective congenital amnesia into the bargain. To be a successful disenfranchised diligent optimist, you are bound to have to tackle incredibly difficult and what often appear to be insurmountable obstacles. If you keep remembering the hurt, the frustration, and the failure, you're likely to stop trying. Forgetfulness can truly be a virtue in these circumstances.

Also, after trying to tackle enough of these challenges by yourself, you begin to understand that you just can't do it alone. In the course of building America and in the course of continuing to build America, we were and are likely to need the help of people with whom we disagree on many subjects. Forgetting those differences so that we can work together to achieve what needs to be achieved has proven to be a very highly successful formula in the New World.

Having this kind of short-term memory is simultaneously useful and dangerous. On the one hand, we do not remember slights and even active combat for very long. That is a good thing because our worst enemies have a way of becoming our best friends. Consider the fact that Japan and Germany are today our greatest trading partners and our most reliable allies. Frankly, in terms of world history, it wasn't that long ago that they were our most despicable enemies.

On the other hand, having such intensely short memories puts us at risk of repeating the same mistakes over and over again. The philosopher George Santayana once said (although the saying has been attributed to many other people also) that those who do not remember history are doomed to repeat it. On the whole, it can be said of Americans that short-term memory has served our best interests more often than not.

Our natural history and our predisposition is to forgive, forget, and get a move on. We tend to forget with astonishing speed and we tend to forgive with incredible ease. Our collective congenital amnesia is one of the most significant reasons for our culture of fresh starts. Our dependable guide to things American, Alexis de Tocqueville, wrote in the 1840s, *They take up and leave 10 different occupations; they do not fear changes, they can enter another activity if the current one does not succeed.* This applies to things in most spheres of Americans' lives.

Forgetting as a first step toward renewal has been part of our makeup from the very beginning. In 1776, Thomas Paine, whose writings had tremendous influence on the American movement toward independence, wrote, *We have it in our power to begin again.* Many years later, President Ronald Reagan used the same quote to pull the country out of a particularly bad economic cycle and onto the road to winning rather than compromising the Cold War.

Americans love nothing more than that concept of fresh starts. The best kind of fresh start is one that leaves behind the baggage of the past. Ralph Waldo Emerson wrote perhaps the most concise and eloquent comment on the seventh marker of the America Code:

Finish each day and be done with it. You have done what you could. Some blunders and absurdities have crept in; forget them as soon as you can. Tomorrow is a new day. You shall begin it serenely and with too high a spirit to be encumbered with your old nonsense.

SECTION III

America's Rich Geopolitical Ecology

THE SEEDS OF THE AMERICAN NATION would not have thrived anywhere else on the planet as they have here. The land itself and the democratic foundations that are defined in and protected by the Declaration of Independence and the Constitution combine to form an environment ideally suited to nurturing the pioneering, adaptive, and expansive culture that is the essence of the America Code.

The physical topography of America is the topography of possibility. From the very beginning, the vast spaces have fostered the immigrant's belief in the ideal of finding "the right spot" just beyond the next hill or mountain or river. Nowhere else does there exist such an astonishing balance of scale, continuity, expansiveness, and promise in a single geography.

There is another kind of topography that made it possible for America to become what it is today. That is the sociopolitical topography defined not by maps but by foundational documents. The Declaration of Independence and the Constitution embody, protect, and preserve the America Code and represent a kind of critical social-political topography. Together they lay out the foundation, rules, and guidelines that make it possible for an ever expanding and changing population to absorb differences of opinion and beliefs yet keep the country moving forward with minimal disruption, keeping it on the same track along which it began.

It is impossible to fully understand the America Code and the American people without appreciating the importance of these cornerstone documents in encouraging it to flourish.

CHAPTER 19

The Land on Which We Have Grown

THERE IS NOTHING SO DEFINING OF A PEOPLE as the topography and the geography from which they spring. You can't talk about the America Code, or the American character, or our historical, political, or social systems without taking note of the stage on which they have all played out and will continue to be played out for decades and centuries to come.

The story of America could not have been told in the same way in any other geography. In the area bounded by "purple mountains' majesty…the fruited plain…spacious skies" and spread "from sea to shining sea," there exists an astonishing balance of scale, continuity, expansiveness, and promise unlike anywhere on earth.

It is equally true that we did not spring from this geography; we migrated to it. Moreover, if we didn't like the particular patch on which we started our American journey, there was, and still is, always another set of possibilities on the road ahead.

That is the first difference between us and our ancestral mind-set—and the reason that we feel not only connected to the land but also that we have the power and the latitude to shape it to our desires or to find more accommodating premises while yet remaining part of this country.

The topography of America is the topography of possibility. No matter where you go in the United States, there is always somewhere else you could be that is thousands of miles away. From the very beginning, the vast spaces fostered an atmosphere in which you could always assume that the right spot for you was beyond the next hill, or the next mountain, or the next river.

It is well worth taking a brief journey across the territory that is also part of the America Code.

CHAPTER 20

On a Grand Scale

ANY WAY YOU SLICE IT, this is a very big country. A really BIG country. Most Americans have little idea just how big it really is. Ranked by land area in square miles, the United States of America comes in third, with roughly 3.7 million square miles. That puts us just below Canada at 3.8 million square miles and a little more than half of Russia's 6.6 million square miles. It also puts us just above China, depending on how you calculate the territory, and while we populate the land with some 300 million Americans, our country is just a bit larger than China with its billion Chinese, and more than twice the land mass of India and its more than one billion Indians.

I have yet to meet a foreign visitor to America who fails to be impressed by the tremendous distances between the East Coast and the West Coast. Foreign visitors to the East Coast are awed by the distances between Boston and Florida. Those visiting the West Coast are likewise amazed by the north/south axis of Washington State down to the tip of Southern California just above the Mexican border, not to mention all that America in between.

This is not surprising since the bulk of European history has taken place in the 900 miles between London and Warsaw or the 1,400 miles between Athens and London. By comparison, it's nearly 1,300 miles from Boston to Miami—and that's just a US seaboard. No wonder the typical tourist response is "What a country!"—usually said with a big grin and an appreciative shake of the head.

CHAPTER 21

Room for Everyone on Planet Earth—Plus

SCALE IS ONE THING. The other important dimension that makes a country work is the relationship between the square miles and the humans living on them. Russia has the single largest landmass of any nation on earth, but its 6.6 million square miles—twice the size of the United States—are inhabited by less than half the number of America's people (150 million vs. America's more than 300 million).

Population density in a country makes a difference in both directions. The nations on earth live in a kind of Goldilocks dynamic. For a given country, the population can be too big, too small, or "just right." If population density is too high, demands against available resources limit progress. If population density is too low, then it's all space and no nation— not enough people to make the geography more than that, geography.

In America's case, the balance of land and people has been just right from the beginning. The people and the landmass of the United States seem to enjoy a happy natural harmony of space and population. The good news is that there is still room to grow and maintain that ideal balance.

The average population density of the world's landmasses is 122 persons per square mile (which makes the planet's land-to-people relationship roughly equal to Lithuania's and twice the density of Ireland). By comparison, the population density of the United States is 83 persons per square mile.

If you were to take the entire population of the globe (some 7 billion people) and relocate them to the United States of America, the new population density of the country (1,842 persons per square mile) would be roughly two-thirds that of the population density of the country of Bangladesh. The new America would be the fifteenth most-densely-populated country on the planet, well behind Macau (18,500), Monaco (16,900), Singapore (7,150), and Hong Kong (6,350), who top the density list of countries... and that's after having absorbed the entire population of planet earth![6]

If you settled the people of the planet—every one of them—instead in just the state of Alaska (with its current population density of 1 person per square mile), Alaska's new population density would be roughly equal to that of the cities of Philadelphia or Boston (roughly 12,000 per square mile)[7] or half that of New York (at nearly 24,000 per square mile).

If the world's population were all brought together in the county of Los Angeles, each person would have a personal living space roughly equal to that of a $4' \times 4'$ standard shower stall, with two Bermudas left over for common space for food service and administration.

This is a country with room and with space to be yourself, and it is likely to stay that way for quite some time to come.

CHAPTER 22

Contiguity – From Sea to Sea and All Points in Between

THE OTHER DIMENSIONS THAT TURN A COMBINATION of geography and people into a force to be reckoned with on the world stage are accessibility and continuity. A people can't get the most from the land they live on unless (a) they can access it and (b) the greatest possible number of citizens can benefit from the greatest access to the nation's resources.

Even in advanced nations such as Russia, Canada, China, India, and Brazil, the largest portions of territory are sparsely populated. In the most remote areas of some of these countries, the population is still leading lives that closely parallel those of our ancestors of one or more generations ago.

What makes the American landscape different from the other large countries on the planet is its unique balance of scale, contiguousness, and accessibility. Virtually every part of America "feels" like a part of America— there is a great sense of continuity across the continent. From sea to shining sea there is a sense of American-ness every step of the way from east to west and from north to south.

This is so partly because Americans carried the America Code to every quarter of the country and partly because the America Code is what it is because the nation was ideally set up for such consolidation of continuity. Within half a century of its founding as a separate nation, the United States had essentially the same continental footprint we see on the map today. On paper, at least, we were a nation that stretched between those shining seas and north to south with roughly today's borders by the middle of the nineteenth century. It was America, primed to be fully populated by Americans.

The settlement of America can be basically divided into quarters. The eastern-most quarter of the country consists mainly of the original thirteen colonies and their "western reserves." Many Americans aren't aware that the original land grants gave some of the original colonies territories that extended due west of their borders. Some of the original grants extended those western reserves as far as the Pacific Ocean. Since none of the new states had the resources to take advantage of their land grants, the colonies ceded those territories to the central government in the course of setting up the United States, thus laying the foundation for what would ultimately become the states of Wisconsin, Michigan, Illinois, Indiana, Ohio, Kentucky, Tennessee, Alabama, Mississippi, and parts of Minnesota (see **Figure 22-1**).

Within fourteen years of its founding, the United States of America basically doubled in size by acquiring the Louisiana Purchase from France—the territories that would eventually make up Montana, North Dakota, the balance of Minnesota, Wyoming, South Dakota, Nebraska, Iowa, Colorado, Kansas, Missouri, Oklahoma, Arkansas, Louisiana, and West Florida.

These were followed shortly with the addition of the rest of Florida as part of Spanish territory ceded in 1819 as well as a land swap with Britain to straighten our northern border at 54 degrees 40 minutes of latitude.

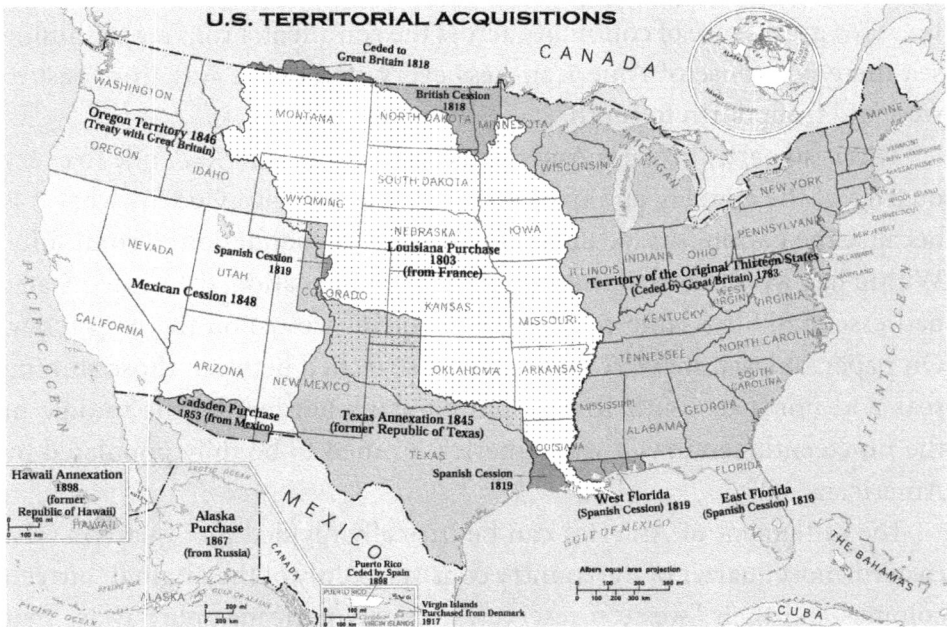

Figure 22-1. Territorial acquisitions of the United States, from *The National Atlas of the United States of America,* provided by the US Department of the Interior.[8]

Between 1845 and 1848, we annexed Texas, got Mexico to cede California, Nevada, Utah, and New Mexico, and got England to yield the territory that would become Washington, Oregon, and Idaho.

No one has ever before (or since) put together so expansive and continuous a geographic nation under a single flag with a single political and social system in so little time. Within some sixty years of the adoption of the US Constitution, America was essentially the America we know today—open for business and ready for population by Americans.

Today it is settled with a remarkably well-distributed population, making the most of virtually every acre to one degree or another (see **Figure 22-2**).

By comparison, 75 percent of Russians continue to make their homes along the western edge of their geography. With all the land available to them, most Canadians congregate along the border with the United States (their southern, our northern, where it is warmer, among other advantages, and where it is easiest to conduct commerce with the "lower fifty"). China, currently the world's most populous country, also makes use of just a fraction of its territory, mainly along the southeastern borders. In the case of most large countries most of the landmass is largely vacant and most of the population sits in one corner or along one edge—which is not the case with America.

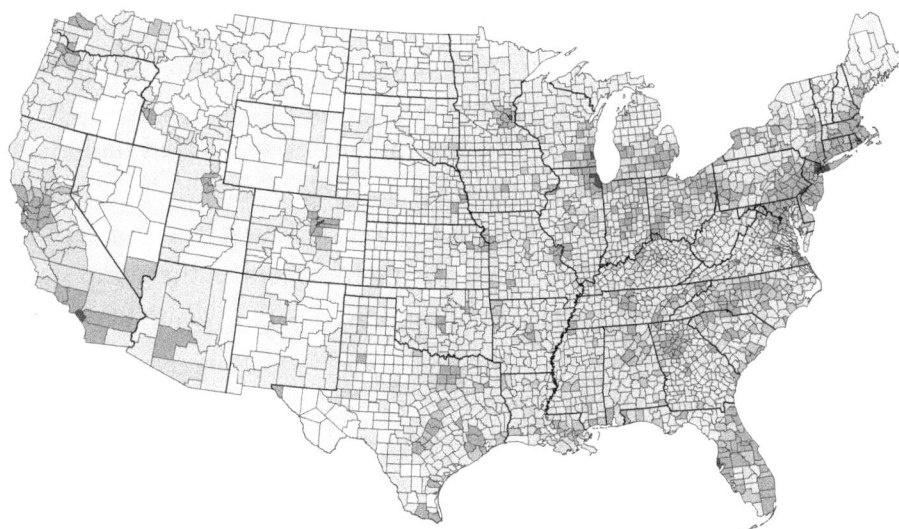

Figure 22-2. US population density. Courtesy the Library of Congress (loc.gov)[9].

In the final analysis, Russia and Canada have more land than we do and fewer people. China has about the same amount of land and more than three times the people we do. Out of these four vast nations, only the United States has managed to distribute its population in an effective connective net from coast to coast and from border to border with something distinctly "American" happening in virtually every inch in between. No place in America is that difficult to get to and no place in America is very far away from the Great American Mainstream.

CHAPTER 23

A Wealth of Blessings

SOCIAL, COMMERCIAL, AND TECHNOLOGICAL PROGRESS depends on access to key raw materials and resources. A people living on a landmass that can barely sustain the population rarely gets beyond rudimentary cultures and societies. Historically, most wars and most conquests have been fueled and justified by a desire of one people to possess the resources that were unavailable within its territories but somehow existed in the lands of their neighbors. From the biblical imperatives of the Hebrews to seize the cities of their neighbors (Jericho, for example) to the global rovings of the Dutch, French, German, Spanish, Italian, Portuguese, English, Arabs, and Norsemen, a shortage of resources and raw materials has led nation after nation to covet and seize from others what it lacked itself.

One of the reasons that America never followed the conventional imperialistic patterns of its predecessors and forebears on the world stage is that the territories we occupy are richly endowed with a wealth of resources and raw materials unequaled on the planet.

Immediately after taking possession of California in 1847, the freshly minted American nation found itself sitting on one of the largest deposits of gold in the world and the rush was on. In a kind of deserved irony, it turned out that Spain (and its Mexican successors in the Americas) had been right to come to the New World seeking gold. Unfortunately for Spain, it was the upstart Americans who in the end would prove to profit from the exercise.

Over the years, we would discover that in every corner of the country were to be found rich storehouses of natural resources. Petroleum in Pennsylvania and the American Southwest, as well as Alaska and off our coastlines. Iron for steel just about everywhere. Coal anywhere you dig down deep enough with a shovel. Not to mention aluminum, uranium, silica, natural gas. You name the resource and we are blessed with it in good to great to extraordinary abundance. Not to mention the rich natural resources of lumber, fish, and game, and an abundance of well-distributed water to irrigate some of the most fertile and productive arable land on the planet.

The truth is that, if the need arose under the worst of circumstances, America is still fully capable of sealing up its borders and creating a self-sustaining, insulated society and economy. Not that this would be a good idea under most circumstances, mind you, but the resources exist if the need required it and the will surfaced to make it so.

There has never been a shortage of building materials. We have always had adequate forests for a variety of uses. In the pre-colonial and colonial era, American lumber proved far superior to Canadian lumber for the production of naval masts (including rare single-piece masts of extraordinary size). This made our country a particularly valuable strategic resource in a world so dependent on navies and vessels of commerce.

Both England and France clearly coveted the high quality and highly abundant wood of America. The simple fact that the English had excluded the French from access to the wood supply of its American colonies was at least part of the reason the French eventually came across the Atlantic to support America's revolution against France's longtime enemy and major competitor on the world stage.

Ask any New England farmer about the availability of construction stone and he would today gladly give you, and would have given throughout our history, as much as you were willing to haul away in clearing his property.

While we are not among the top sources of oil in the world, America has an estimated 100 years' supply of natural gas at current production levels.[10] Proven oil and gas reserves are equivalent to around 46–60 and 100 years, respectively, at current production levels.

Coal reserves are available in almost every country worldwide, with recoverable reserves in about seventy countries. The biggest reserves are in the United States, Russia, China, and India. After centuries of mineral exploration, the location, size, and characteristics of most countries' coal resources are quite well known. What tends to vary much more than the assessed level of the resource—that is, the potentially accessible coal in the ground—is the level classified as proved recoverable reserves. The United States has the largest proved reserves of any country on earth. In fact, America has 27 percent of the world's proved coal reserves. It has been estimated that there are over 847 billion tons of proved coal reserves worldwide. This means that there is enough coal to last us Americans another 119 years at current rates of production.

The United States is the tenth-largest producer of iron ore[11] and the fourth-largest producer of hydroelectric power in the world.[12]

All in all, if we had to rely on our own natural resources we could maintain a continuing independence from the rest of the world. True, such a drastic policy change would require major restructuring of how we produce and use those resources, but the fundamental capacity is there.

CHAPTER 24

Pickup Rules of Engagement for a Nation

THE SOCIOPOLITICAL ECOLOGY OF AMERICAN DEMOCRACY is at least as important as the country's geography or physical topography in defining what makes America America and Americans Americans. The one thing that can be said about the people of this country, going back to the beginning, is that on the whole we would really rather have things in writing. While we gladly offer our handshake as a binding contract between two Americans, the relationship between the citizen and the government has always been a matter of the written word here.

Many people don't realize that even to this day the United Kingdom has no written constitution. It functions as a kind of "gentlemen's agreement" model where best intentions are presumed—although often proved not to be such. Americans, on the other hand, having experienced the vagaries and caprices of King George III, insist on spelling everything out with an absolute minimum of equivocation and a minimum of assumption. That is why our social and political system is grounded in two incredible and far-seeing documents.

The Declaration of Independence is an almost painfully detailed enumeration of the various malfeasances, misfeasances, and nonfeasances perpetrated by the British Crown against its American subjects, acts that forced our hand toward separation. Its authors believed in the importance of explaining in minute detail why that separation was not only fully justified but necessary.

The Constitution took that thinking forward and defined what is essentially a strategic plan for the whole nation. It sets out the purpose for getting together as a nation. It defines who is responsible for doing what. It lays out a road map for how the various parts work together to create and maintain the nation. The evidence suggests after 250 years that it *was* a good plan, still *is* a good plan, and there's no reason it can't serve as a map and touchstone for the journey ahead.

Most importantly, the Constitution clearly identifies what is the natural order of things in the way of human rights, and it places very specific limitations on what government can do, should do, and must do. At the same time it expressly indicates that if the government of the Republic is not given or assigned a specific right, it does not possess that right.

As far as I can see, there is very little ambiguity in either of these foundational documents and not nearly as much room for interpretation as has been presumed over the years. A close reading insists that what lawyers and judges might view as unclear is quite definitive in terms of language and certainly all the more definitive when considered within the circumstances and the moment of authorship.

In a sense, the Constitution operates as a set of pickup game rules for the nation. According to Wikipedia, pickup rules in sports are basic, minimal, essential, flexible, and dependent on trust: "Without formal rules and regulations, pick-up games are often played with a looser set of rules which are sometimes established by the players themselves." First, as in a pickup basketball game, the Constitution's rules for turning a collection of separate colonies into a nation were established by the "players themselves." Having no clear guidelines or precedents, the Founders pretty much made them up as they went along, creating a document that provided for that process to continue. Secondly, the constitutional rules are significantly "looser" than the British legal mandates from which we separated ourselves.

Most importantly, the rules are clear about the intent to empower only that which needs to be empowered. The British Crown had vested in it all rights except those proscribed by Magna Carta and such. Our American foundational documents, on the other hand, vested in the central government only those powers that were specifically spelled out in the Constitution. The difference between the two approaches is huge in that the power of the government is strictly limited in the case of the Constitution and effectively unlimited in the case of the English monarchy—and that's the way Americans wanted it to be from the very beginning.

Most of what I understand about the Declaration of Independence and the Constitution comes secondhand at best. I had read both documents at one point or another in my past, but I never really READ either of them intensely and literally until relatively recently. Like many Americans, over the years, I've seen the Constitution and the Declaration through the prism of not-quite-totally disinterested parties. If you look at the original documents themselves, you quickly realize that they say nothing about "separation of powers" or "separation of church and state." Those phrases were supplied by people whose purpose it was to "clarify" and explain what the authors *intended* rather than what they actually said.

The good news is that it isn't very difficult to pick up the original documents (at least copies of them), read for yourself what the Founders wrote, and come to your own conclusions about what they did or did not intend through the language they chose. The Founders of the United States were plain-speaking folks—certainly when compared to the verbiage-generators who followed and continually insist on recasting and explaining what those men "meant to say."

Somebody once said that anybody who says "in other words" probably didn't get the statement right in the first place. I don't think that's the case with the authors of our foundational documents. I believe they knew what they were about. They understood a lot better than we why these documents needed to be written and they were quite clear about what they meant to say in relatively simple, minimalist text.

Of the three documents discussed below, the first is the Declaration of Independence itself, because neither of the subsequent American documents would ever have happened without the Declaration. The second document is the Letter of Transmittal that went with the Constitution, because it's the framework within which the authors of that Constitution had to work to create the document. In that sense, it is almost more important than the Constitution itself in appreciating why what happened happened and what the document was meant to do for the newly minted United States of America. The third text, the Constitution of the United States of America, is equally articulate in establishing the "why" of America and should be understood in its own context and in its own time, not only through the prism of innumerable subsequent interpretations.

It also helps if you understand what matters (and mattered at the time) to most Americans and how they value (and valued) what they value. Those insights tend to cast our foundational documents as a simpler, less convoluted set of texts.

With all that as preamble, let's take a look at what was actually written back there between 1775 and 1790. In each case, the plan is to highlight the most significant issues and rethink them on the merits of the original language and the context of the times alone. I am neither a judicial scholar nor a lawyer, but I have a healthy respect for and appreciation of language and how it works. It is with that perspective that we go into the next several chapters.

CHAPTER 25

The Declaration –
The Unlearned Layman's Reading

A PERSONAL PLEA AND A PIECE OF ADVICE: Promise yourself that you will make the time to read the whole document. All Americans owe it to themselves. I guarantee you'll be glad you did (see **Figure 25-1**).

The most striking thing about the Declaration of Independence is how civil and polite a document it is. This is astonishing considering that its authors potentially put themselves under the penalty of execution for treason by writing, signing, and publicly proclaiming it. It comprises 1,458 words.

The second remarkable thing about this document is how (almost painfully) it details the malfeasances, misfeasances, and nonfeasances of King George III as justification for the Great American Separation. Unlike the initiators of the French Revolution, which followed some thirteen years later, we were not assaulting the throne in our midst. Instead, we were simply ratifying the factual separation (by sheer distance at the very least—in the mid-1700s, it took as much as fifteen weeks at sea to get to America from Europe and 10 percent or more of the travelers died during the journey[13]) between the American colonies and the mother country.

Let's tackle the Declaration one key part at a time.

I can't think of a more respectful rationale for something as drastic as challenging the most powerful empire on earth at the time than this beginning:

> *When in the Course of human events, it becomes necessary for one people to dissolve the political bands which have connected them with another, and to assume among the powers of the earth, the separate and equal station to which the Laws of Nature and of Nature's God entitle them, a decent respect to the opinions of mankind requires that they should declare the causes which impel them to the separation.*

Americans were most courteous even in their very first act as Americans. We all know about the "certain unalienable rights," which include

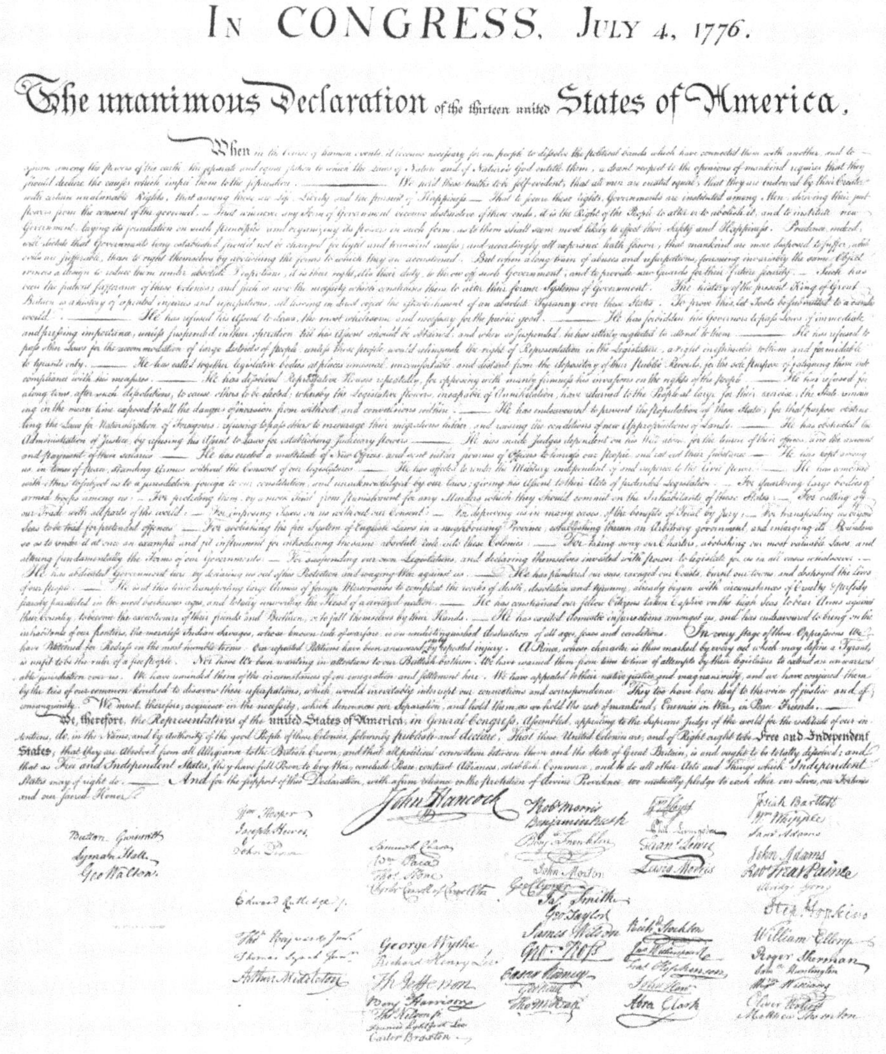
IN CONGRESS, JULY 4, 1776.

The unanimous Declaration of the thirteen united States of America,

Figure 25-1. The Declaration of Independence.

an absolute guarantee of life and liberty but only the opportunity to *pursue* happiness. Not only not an entitlement but specifically an offer of opportunity or possibility, which it bears saying represented an incredible leap forward in individual liberty for the time... and well beyond for much of the rest of the world.

Then the declaration goes on, and on, and on about the grievances perpetrated by an individual (George III) against the American colonies. The Declaration makes things rather personal and treats the English monarch as a petty and disparaging person.

The history of the present King of Great Britain is a history of repeated injuries and usurpations, all having in direct object the establishment of an absolute Tyranny over these States. To prove this, let Facts be submitted to a candid world.

The list of "injuries and usurpations" begins with the king's refusal to allow the passage of colonial laws for the good of the colonies and goes on to list an additional twenty-six grievances that impelled the separation, including such small stuff as setting up meetings when and where the delegates were least likely to attend and wearing them down by delaying in every way possible the seating of legislatures and the appointment of officials. The king was also accused of actively trying to keep Americans few in number by unreasonably obstructing the naturalization of immigrants. He was also guilty of sending cronies to make their fortunes at the colonials' expense—the original pork barrel plan for politicians.

Most notably, the Declaration makes it clear that it was not we who separated ourselves from England because "He has abdicated Government here, by declaring us out of his Protection and waging War against us."

As the Founders saw it, England abandoned us long before we left it. Here is a prime example of the other side of the *pragmatic combatants* factor. Having thoroughly outlined the reasons and cited innumerable examples of abuses suffered, the Declaration, with impeccable logic, leads inexorably toward the only reasonable, rationale, prudent, and pragmatic solution—a separation from England and the devising of a new set of rules between the governed and the governors.

CHAPTER 26

The Letter of Transmittal – The Unlearned Layman's Reading

PLEASE PROMISE ME, and yourself, that you will make the time to read the whole document, please! (See **Figure 26-1**.)

If you want a peek inside the mind of the Foundational Americans (who also happen to be Archetypal Americans), this document is a perfect place to start. It is the brilliant expression of the America Code at work, touching on each of the code's markers in turn.

It is clearly the work of disenfranchised diligent optimists who are addicted to individual liberty and dedicated to the principle of possibility, who have created the letter and the Constitution it introduces as an act of association rather than consensus. Moreover, it clearly pronounces that the state is not to be trusted. Finally, its very existence rests on the principle of pragmatism and is grounded in an intentional act of collective amnesia in that it proposes the necessity of creating something new in the way of government, without regard to the traditions that preceded it.

While a lot of people have actually read and attempted to understand the Constitution of the United States, a significantly smaller number have made the time to read the document that introduced it to the Continental Congress in 1787. This is the note that the authors of the Constitution attached to the draft submitted to that Congress.

The note itself is revealing about how Americans go about getting even the most important things done. You would expect that so significant a document as the new constitution of a new model for a new country would have been presented with a great deal of flourish, fanfare, and grandiosity, not to mention the intense personal pride of having created a landmark document for the ages. That is clearly not the tone nor the content of the Letter of Transmittal.

In Convention September 17, 1787

Sir,

We have now the honor to submit to the consideration of the United States in Congress assembled, that Constitution which has appeared to us the most advisable.

The friends of our country have long seen and desired, that the power of making war, peace, and treaties, that of levying money and regulating commerce, and the correspondent executive and judicial authorities should be fully and effectually vested in the general government of the Union: But the impropriety of delegating such extensive trust to one body of men is evident—Hence results the necessity of a different organization.

It is obviously impractical in the federal government of these states, to secure all rights of independent sovereignty to each, and yet provide for the interest and safety of all: Individuals entering into society, must give up a share of liberty to preserve the rest. The magnitude of the sacrifice must depend as well on situation and circumstances, as on the object to be obtained. It is at all times difficult to draw with precision the line between those rights which must be surrendered, and those which may be reserved; and on the present occasion this difficulty was encreased by a difference among the several states as to their situation, extent, habits, and particular interests.

In all our deliberations on this subject we kept steadily in our view, that which appears to us the greatest interest of every true American, the consolidation of our Union, in which is involved our prosperity, felicity, safety, perhaps our national existence. This important consideration, seriously and deeply impressed on our minds, led each state in the Convention to be less rigid on points of inferior magnitude, than might have been otherwise expected; and thus the Constitution, which we now present, is the result of a spirit of amity, and of that mutual deference and concession which the peculiarity of our political situation rendered indispensable.

That it will meet the full and entire approbation of every state is not perhaps to be expected; but each will doubtless consider that had her interest been alone consulted, the consequences might have been particularly disagreeable or injurious to others; that it is liable to as few exceptions as could reasonably have been expected, we hope and believe; that it may promote the lasting welfare of that country so dear to us all, and secure her freedom and happiness, is our most ardent wish.

With great respect, We have the honor to be, Sir,
Your Excellency's most obedient and humble servants,

George Washington, President
By unanimous Order of the Convention.
His Excellency, the President of Congress

Figure 26-1. Transcription of the Letter of Transmittal

It begins rather modestly:

In Convention September 17, 1787

Sir,

We have now the honor to submit to the consideration of the United States in Congress assembled, that Constitution which has appeared to us the most advisable.

"Most advisable" is a long, long way from ideal, or perfect, or even definitive. It signals from the very beginning that the document is the product of accommodation and pragmatism. The pragmatic and realistic nature of the document becomes even clearer in the next paragraph:

The friends of our country have long seen and desired, that the power of making war, peace, and treaties, that of levying money and regulating commerce, and the correspondent executive and judicial authorities should be fully and effectually vested in the general government of the Union: But the impropriety of delegating such extensive trust to one body of men is evident—Hence results the necessity of a different organization.

This "different organization" is what is generally referred to as the "separation of powers." As the letter is written, however, the purpose is a great deal less lofty. You don't have to read between the lines too carefully to discern what the authors originally intended. Remember that these men had just gotten rid of an autocrat for whom they had developed the most intense distrust and dislike. At the outset, they wanted to make sure that never again in our national history would any one individual or organization be trusted (they literally insisted on "the impropriety of . . . such extensive trust").

They also never mentioned anything about the concept of "checks and balances," which is so associated with the idea of separation of powers— fine words indeed, but interpretations and shadings of which the original authors were not guilty. What they said, based plainly and directly on a paraphrase of Lord Acton's memorable observation that "Power tends to corrupt and absolute power corrupts absolutely,"[14] is that government is not to be trusted! They purposely set up an obstructionist mechanism so as to weaken and dissipate the power of the federal government. They might have said it more succinctly as "In ONE we do not trust!"

They did go on to note that the draft document was not exactly the superb result of amicable unanimity—not by a long shot:

> _That it will meet the full and entire approbation of every state is not perhaps to be expected_; but each will doubtless consider that had her interest been alone consulted, the consequences might have been particularly disagreeable or injurious to others; _that it is liable to as few exceptions as could reasonably have been expected_, we hope and believe; that it may promote the lasting welfare of that country so dear to us all, and secure her freedom and happiness, is our most ardent wish.

The two underlined phrases make it clear that the document was the product of accommodations and compromises that made the smallest number of participants unhappy. Even at so critical a juncture in our brand-new history, everybody held on to independence and yielded it only grudgingly as a matter of necessity. That is why the final document required the approval of only nine of the thirteen states for ratification.

CHAPTER 27

The Constitution — A Layman's Reading

PLEASE PROMISE ME AND YOURSELF that you will make the time to read the whole document, please (see **Figure 27-1**).

…and that brings us to the Big Kahuna of foundational documents, the Constitution of the United States of America. These folks got a chance to invent a whole new way of doing business as a country. The odds are that their invention would inherently reflect the nature of the authors. This the Constitution does—brilliantly! The context for this document is not only the moment in time at which it was written; it is also a reflection of

Figure 27-1. The Constitution of the United States of America. Courtesy the Library of Congress (loc.gov).

the fundamentally different view of the relationship between government and the governed held by a people who chose to actively separate from the home country that spawned them. The Constitution is the product of the America Code, which is precisely what made it, and continues to make it, the basis for a different kind of nation.

That, perhaps, is the most meaningful insight that connects the Constitution to the America Code. It explains why the document intentionally defines a new balance between an individual, a "state," and a central government. Because of our addiction to individual liberty, the Constitution turns the traditional mind-set upside down, literally. For the first time in history, the people specify the terms under which they expect to be governed. Because government is not to be trusted, it is divided and set against itself through the separation of powers: the last thing the authors wanted was a strong, centralized form of government. Furthermore, because individual liberty is paramount, the role of the central government is strictly limited. The central authority is to do only that which it is assigned to do. In the European system we left behind, monarchs had carte blanche to do whatever they believed right.

The Constitution begins with a crystal clear statement of purpose, remembered for a short moment by American kids about to take a test on the subject of the Constitution and more honored in its forgetting than remembering by the majority of American adults:

> *We the People of the United States, in Order to form a more perfect Union, establish Justice, insure domestic Tranquility, provide for the common defence, promote the general Welfare, and secure the Blessings of Liberty to ourselves and our Posterity, do ordain and establish this Constitution for the United States of America.*

After that resounding opening, the Constitution immediately devolves into Article One, the painfully detailed descriptions of Congress, its duties, and its makeup. Then follows Article Two, which does the same for the executive, and Article Three for the judiciary. Article Four outlines the way in which the states interact with one another and with "the Union"—again in great detail and with a total of 4,543 words in its unamended original. (For comparison, the Christian Bible contains 774,746 words and the US Tax Code more than SEVEN MILLION!) Article Five proposes that changes to the Constitution be made through amendments. Article Six insists on oaths of support but specifically excludes any religious test as a qualification for holding public office. Article Seven basically establishes that only nine states are required for ratification (recognizing that even this perfect document might not meet everyone's approbation, although it was finally ratified by all thirteen).

By implication and general understanding at the time, what is not specifically mentioned in this brief document as appropriate to the Union remains the province of the individual states. Brevity is exclusive rather than inclusive in terms of what the Union can and should do to fulfill the requirements of the Preamble. The America Code at work!

In support of this point of view is the fact that from the moment of its inception, amendments were added to clarify and ensure the rights of the states and the rights of individual Americans in some detail. It is no accident that the First Amendment reads:

Congress shall make no law respecting an establishment of religion, or prohibiting the free exercise thereof; or abridging the freedom of speech, or of the press, or the right of the people peaceably to assemble, and to petition the Government for a redress of grievances.

The Constitution's position on the various rights of freedom of speech, the press, and peaceful assembly to redress grievances is perfectly clear. So why has the conversation about religion become so fuzzy? Once again, the original document says nothing about "separation of church and state." Mainly because that was never the intent. Given the intolerable dominance of the Church of England and its influence on the English system of government at the time, what the authors wanted was that there should be no single state religion lording it over the others.

The second phrase about no law "prohibiting the free exercise [of religion]" is telling. If there is any implication to be derived from the Constitution's language about separation of church and state, there is equally as much argument that the original intention was inclusive and meant to ensure the ongoing relationship between God and man. It is a matter of uncomfortable irony that later interpretations are in direct contradiction to this original intent. It can be reasonably argued that secularism is a belief system on a par with other belief systems (religions). It cannot be argued that secularism is the benchmark from which religious preferences differ. What has happened is that the legal precedents have given a priority to the belief system that is secularism and put its values above those of others.

The Ninth and Tenth Amendments clearly state that any power that is not specifically invested in the Union continues to remain in the hands of either the people or the various states. According to the Constitution, there is no vacuum for the central government to fill—ever! The text is crystal clear on these points.

Amendment IX

The enumeration in the Constitution of certain rights shall not be construed to deny or disparage others retained by the people.

Amendment X

The powers not delegated to the United States by the Constitution, nor prohibited by it to the States, are reserved to the States respectively, or to the people.

The rest of the amendments (Eleven through Twenty-Seven) cover a range of issues we needed to address as a nation over the past 250 years. These ranged from the right of women to act as full citizens to issues of slavery and civil rights, not to mention the abolition and reinstatement of American recreational drinking (the Eighteenth Amendment taketh away, and the Twenty-First Amendment giveth back).

The most recent amendment (originally proposed unsuccessfully in 1789 and finally ratified in 1992!) was a reminder to the members of Congress that they should be both prudent and reasonable in not voting themselves raises that take effect during the terms in which they vote.

Precisely because it is not weighed down by the dreadful weight of detail that characterizes the US Tax Code, the Constitution can serve as the framework rather than the dictum for how we continue to get along and work toward keeping this Union alive, viable, and functioning smoothly into the future. For that to happen, we need to free ourselves from an unrealistic insistence on finding consensus and embrace the positive obstructionism and dissension enshrined in the America Code.

SECTION IV

Less Melting Pot than Cocktail

AMERICA IS A NATION OF MINORITIES—a marvelous cocktail of nationalities where a variety of beliefs and opinions come together yet maintain their distinct flavors. What makes America work is that every nationality contributes to the impact of the whole without losing its own special qualities. A conformity that eliminates differences and erodes nuances has no place in a code based on the concepts of democracy, individualism, liberty, and initiative.

As a marketer I have made a career of studying Americans and how they think and act. In the process, I have discovered patterns of thinking and behavior that help explain why a people who share the same basic code on the one hand can have diametrically opposed ways of thinking and acting on the other. These patterns also help to explain why we as a nation can get into trouble despite the overall optimistic and innovative mind-set of the America Code.

It is a documentable fact that nearly 50 percent of Americans consistently disagree with the other nearly 50 percent. Understanding why we can do that and still hold together as a nation is key to understanding America's upswings, downswings, and digressions and to providing a platform for understanding how we can better take those shifts in stride.

CHAPTER 28

A Nation of Minorities

NOW THAT WE HAVE SPENT ALL THIS TIME framing out the "archetypal" American, it's time to put together the rest of the story. If we are all one people, why do we so often disagree so intensely? Why do we often seem to speak with many voices rather than with one? The answer is in the numbers.

In the 2000 US census, just 7.2 percent of those surveyed identified themselves as "American," which means that more than 82 percent of Americans are connected enough to their own national backgrounds to still identify with them. Remember that "American" was one of the available choices for every respondent in the census—and more than eight out of ten chose not to use that option.

According to the 2000 census, the top ten national origins of Americans are, in descending order, German, Irish, English, American, Mexican, Italian, Polish, French, Scottish, and Dutch—each of which comprises a population of 8 million or more. Any of these hyphenated American groups could be a nation in its own right (see **Table 28-1**).

The relative percentages of total mother-country population compared to American-immigrated population are also illuminating. The total number of Irish-Americans is *six times* the number of the Irish in Ireland. There is one Scottish-American for every Scot. There are half as many German-Americans as there are Germans in Germany. There is one English-American for every two Englishmen. There are one-fourth as many Dutch, Italian, and Polish Americans as there are Dutch, Italians, and Poles in their own country. There are one-sixth as many Mexican Americans as there are Mexicans. The fascinating observation is that there are fewer Americans in America than there are members of the top nationalities in America (see **Table 28-2**).

Table 28-1. Top 10 National Origins of Americans

Top 10 National Origins of Americans	Percentage of US Total	Millions	Aggregate Percentage of US
1. German	15.2	42.8	15.2
2. Irish	10.8	30.5	26.0
3. English	7.7	24.5	33.7
4. American	7.2	20.2	40.9
5. Mexican	6.5	18.4	47.4
6. Italian	5.6	15.6	53.0
7. Polish	3.2	9.0	56.2
8. French	3.2	8.3	59.4
9. Scottish	1.7	4.9	61.1
10. Dutch	1.6	4.5	62.7
TOTAL		**178.7**	**62.7**

Table 28-2. Comparison of Nationalities in America versus Home Countries			
Nationality	In Home Country	In USA	Percentage of Mother Country
Ireland	4,600,000	30,500,000	665.8
Scotland	5,200,000	4,900,000	94.2
Germany	81,800,000	42,800,000	52.3
England	62,400,000	29,400,000	47.1
Netherlands	16,700,800	4,500,000	27.0
Italy	60,00,000	15,600,000	25.7
Poland	38,200,000	9,000,000	23.6
Mexico	112,300,000	18,400,000	16.4
France	65,800,000	8,300,000	12.6
America	312,000,000	22,464,000	7.2

CHAPTER 29

A Lot More Pluribus than Unum

"OUT OF MANY, ONE"—well, not exactly!

I grew up as a Polish kid living next door to the Irish church that I never attended and passing the Italian church in the neighborhood on my way to the Polish church. Having had that experience, I am intimately aware of how we can all be "unum" as Americans, but also continue to be "pluribus" in the plural.

The unique thing about America (and I believe this to be part of what makes Americans Americans) is that there is no central majority, just a lot of different, splintered us's.

The list below, from the 2010 census, shows only those American ancestries with populations of more than 1 million. The largest (German) is just over 15 percent of our total population. The smallest (Vietnamese) is less than one-half of 1 percent.

Note that while marketers and demographers talk about "Hispanics" and "Latinos" as a single group, respondents to the census describe themselves with finer distinctions centering on nationalities, such as Mexican (6.5 percent), Puerto Rican (0.9 percent), Spanish (0.8 percent), Cuban (0.4 percent)...and a lot of other descriptions connected with nationhood rather than "Hispanic-ness" (see **Table 29-1**).

And that's just the national ethnicities with at least a million members!

Table 29-1. Population Statistics of 37 Ethnic Groups in the United States					
National Ancestry[15]	Total	Percentage of US population	National Ancestry[15]	Total	Percentage of US population
1. German	42,841,569	15.2	20. French Canadian	2,349,684	0.8
2. Irish	30,524,799	10.8	21. Chinese	2,271,562	0.8
3. African-American*	24,903,412	8.8	22. Spanish	2,187,144	0.8
4. English	24,509,692	8.7	23. Filipino	2,116,478	0.8
5. American	20,188,305	7.2	24. European	1,968,696	0.7
6. Mexican	18,382,291	6.5	25. Welsh	1,753,794	0.6
7. Italian	15,638,348	5.6	26. Asian Indian	1,546,703	0.5
8. Polish	8,977,235	3.2	27. Danish	1,430,897	0.5
9. French	8,309,666	3.0	28. Hungarian	1,398,702	0.5
10. American Indian*	7,876,568	2.8	29. Czech	1,258,452	0.4
11. Scottish	4,890,581	1.7	30. Korean	1,190,353	0.4
12. Dutch	4,541,770	1.6	31. African	1,183,316	0.4
13. Norwegian	4,477,725	1.6	32. Portuguese	1,173,691	0.4
14. Other ancestries	4,380,380	1.6	33. Greek	1,153,295	0.4
15. Scot-Irish	4,319,232	1.5	34. Japanese	1,103,325	0.4
16. Swedish	3,998,310	1.4	35. Cuban	1,097,594	0.4
17. Puerto Rican	2,652,598	0.9	36. British	1,085,718	0.4
18. Russian	2,652,214	0.9	37. Vietnamese	1,029,420	0.4
19. Hispanic	2,451,109	0.9			

*Not strictly identifiable nationalities. Included as pro forma populations.

CHAPTER 30

How Half of America Is Coded to Disagree

IT'S THE FIFTY PERCENT CONUNDRUM. If you go to Google or one of the other Internet search engines and type in the words "50 percent of Americans + poll," you will find an incredible number of returns that basically confirm that 50 percent of Americans are generally unlikely to agree with the other 50 percent of Americans.

Furthermore, if you take a historical perspective on the same issue, you will find that throughout most of our history, half of America thinks one way and the other half thinks either in a diametrically opposed or simply a different way.

Why would that be? If we believe that the America Code is what makes Americans Americans, shouldn't most of us think the same way on most issues? Shouldn't we usually agree on most questions? There are a number of answers to that question, the first of which is that not all Americans are equally disenfranchised diligent optimists with collective congenital amnesia, etc. But that is only the beginning.

While it is true that America has a higher than average density of disenfranchised diligent optimists compared to any place else, it does not naturally follow that every American is a DDO. And there are a number of ways in which we can be both differentiated and divided and still be one people. As I discussed in "A Nation by Nuances, Halves, and Trichotomies," which is based on evidence, not generally available, from my own original research, just under half of Americans are essentially proactive by nature, another roughly equal number are essentially inactive—with a small but critical reactive minority siding with one side or the other at different moments in time and on different issues.

Would that it were only that simple. According to my original research, there are actually eight ways to make decisions and value things in America. I call these ways "cultureographies" and they are described below.

CHAPTER 31

Eight American Cultureographies

AFTER SOME THIRTY-FIVE YEARS OF PROFESSIONAL INVESTIGATION into how people make decisions and how they value what they value, and based on a proprietary research methodology known as the Index of What Matters Most—with more than 35,000 respondents researched—I have developed a detailed and *cultureographically* nuanced view of eight different types of Americans. Each type makes decisions differently from the others, values what it values in different ways, and communicates in a lexicon all its own.

At the voting booth, in the workforce, or in the marketplace, America's population includes four proactive cultureographic segments labeled *Advocates, Sophisticates, Conventionals,* and *Mechanists.* There are also three inactive segments labeled *Students, Caretakers,* and *Indulgents.* Finally there is also a group called *Gradualists,* who under different circumstances take sides with some groups over others but rarely in a consistent manner.

The first four cultureographic groups, who are essentially proactive, comprise about 44 percent of all Americans. The second set of three groups, who are essentially inactive, comprise 46 percent. The last group, the Gradualists, are fundamentally reactive and make up the remaining 10 percent of the population. These folks can go either way depending on circumstances—which makes them difficult as customers and powerful as voters.

Based on the Gradualists' decisions at any moment in time, the pendulum could swing in either direction on any issue. In fact, one interesting dynamic among these groups is that they are, and have apparently always been, in a delicate equilibrium that keeps the country from moving too far in any particular direction for any extended period of time. Gradualists are part of the great American centering counterweight and the force that has kept America on an even keel for most of our national history.

CHAPTER 32

Not Exactly One and All

WHILE THERE IS, ON THE ONE HAND, such a thing as a decidedly American character, there is also, on the other hand, a shortage of explanations for the inconsistencies in that character. Perhaps the most obvious question is why nearly half of Americans fail to vote in presidential elections, let alone the even lower turnout for off-year elections. If we Americans were consistently of one stripe, then we would all, naturally enough, either always vote or never vote. That is not the way it works in the real world.

For some of us, enjoying the full benefits of being an American and recognizing that those benefits were hard-won through the sacrifices of others, it is inconceivable that anyone would take a pass at the voting booth. What kind of people can actively exclude themselves from the most historically important political process in the country?

What makes it possible for us to be Americans one and all and at the same time be so distinctly divided in one of the most significant things that makes us Americans in the first place? To answer that question, I have developed a way to dimensionalize the complete decisioning system of individuals and groups by identifying *micro values systems* (the context within which they make decisions), quantifying their *lexicon* (the way they understand specific words, ideas, and symbols), and deciphering their change vectors (a kind of "pre-trend" that shows us the intensity and direction of change or where things are going rather than where they have been).

The most fascinating outcome of the research is that there appear to be eight fundamentally different ways of looking at and making your way in the world. There are indications that the eight fundamental cultureographies exist in all nations—although the relative proportions of the groups will be significantly different. In this book we are concerned only with what goes on in America. It is equally true that the eight distinctions occur within each American ethnic group, where, too, they may differ in relative proportions from group to group.

The chart below shows the eight different cultureographies that were originally developed for marketing and advertising purposes. Over time, the model has proven to provide an excellent appreciation for understanding the differences between people in general and Americans in particular.

There are several things that should be clarified before getting too far into this discussion. While the following distinctions may appear a bit simplistic, they have helped our clients to do better marketing, to better manage and motivate the people who work for them, and in many cases to better deal with children, spouses, and other family members. They have been market-tested and they work. That is why this line of thinking may also explain how Americans are similar yet different and how that might translate into behavior in the voting booth and the political process as a whole—why limit to political behavior? After all, this method started out as a marketing/economic tool. Seems it would apply to almost any sector.

While some people fall neatly into one of the following categories, most of us will find that we relate to one of the following groups as a primary classification and also exhibit some factors from a secondary classification.

CHAPTER 33

American Cultureographies — The Big Picture

THE FOUR PROACTIVE AMERICAN CULTUREOGRAPHIES and their percentage of the total population are listed in **Table 33-1**. These are the people who take the initiative and who get things done. They push for their ideas. Proactives fall on all sides of every social and political issue; it is their diligence and energy that keeps America moving forward. In a sense, these four types of proactives form the subgroups of our disenfranchised diligent optimists.

The three inactive American cultureographies are also outlined in **Table 33-1**. Inactives are the people who are along for the ride in America. They contribute by way of labor and consumption. They are essential to the functioning of America but do not actively participate in directing it.

Table 33-1. American Cultureographies					
Proactive Americans		**Inactive Americans**		**Reactive Americans**	
Advocates	8%	Students	10%	Gradualists	10%
Sophisticates	10%	Caretakers	18%		
Conventionals	9%	Indulgents	18%		
Mechanists	17%				
Total	**44%**	**Total**	**46%**	**Total**	**10%**

The good news is that, in America, the 80/20 rule does not apply. While there are more inactive Americans than proactive Americans, the margin is small at 46 percent vs. 44 percent.

The third type, reactives, are the real power base in America although they comprise only 10 percent of the total population (see **Table 33-1**). This is because proactive and inactive values systems in America are at a virtual standoff in most American elections. Roughly 50 percent of Americans don't vote and the proactives, who do, divide roughly 50/50. It's interesting to note that, regardless of the numerical advantage of registered Democrats (72 million registered) to Republicans (55 million registered), presidential elections come close to being self-canceling exercises for the major political parties. There is just about one Republican vote for every Democratic vote actually cast. The tie-breakers, the deciding factor in most elections, come from the pool of American Gradualists.

CHAPTER 34

Cultureography – An Original Model

From marketing assignment to social analysis (see **Figure 34-1**).

ADVOCATES (8 PERCENT)

AS CONSUMERS, Advocates are those customers who, once they discover you or your product, have a natural propensity to tell one and all about your wonderfulness. Marketers believe that they want every consumer to be an

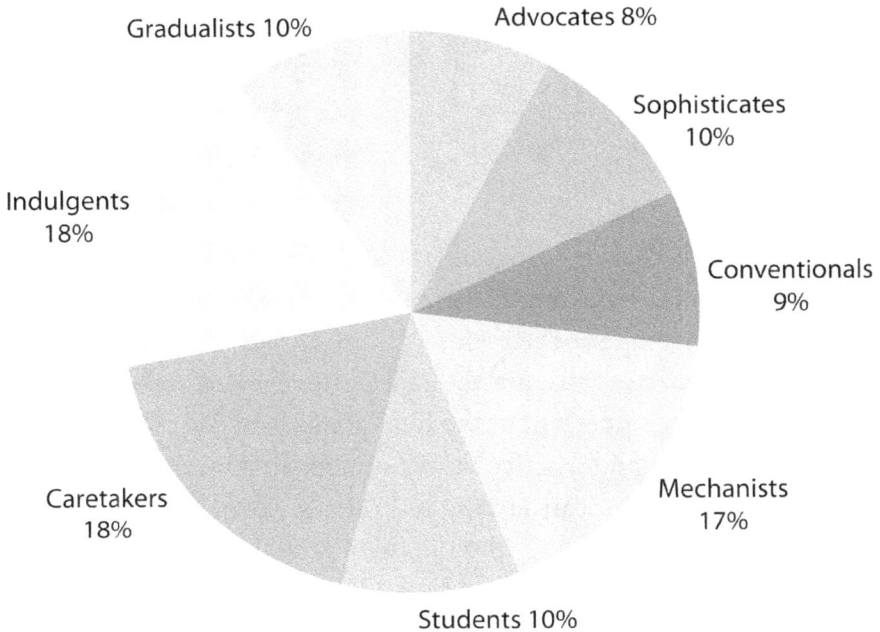

Figure 34-1. Percentages of the total population represented by each of the eight American Culturographies.

advocate for their brand. But there is a dark side to the Advocate consumer. Once they have taken you on as their personal project, they will hold you to their highest standards and expectations. Woe to the marketer who fails a constituency of Advocates. Advocates tend to invest even greater energy into telling others about your failure than they do about your success.

In politics, as in all things, Advocates can't help themselves. Once they perceive "the" truth (because advocates tend to see only one truth—theirs), they simply must enlighten everyone else. Advocates assume that everyone either does, or must, believe what they believe. When two Advocates engage, advocating opposite sides of the same issue, it is total warfare. For an Advocate, it is not enough that you accept what they believe. Until you completely and unreservedly believe what they believe, you are nothing less than pernicious in your denial and defiance. If you are not with them, you are wrong and you are against what is right.

Advocates begin to exercise their political influence long before they enter the voting booth. In fact, "influence" is their elemental goal. Regardless of the issue, for Advocates there is only one side—the correct side, whatever side they believe in, their side, the side of all reasonable people. Casting their own vote is a minor exercise. Influencing correct thinking in others is by far more important.

The thing to remember about each of these eight types, whether you're seeing them as voters or customers (or employees or members of your family, for that matter) is that you should work with who they are. Expecting every customer to become an Advocate is likely to alienate the 92 percent of the population who are not. Sending information to Students is a great idea only if you are in the information business and you can get them to pay you for that information; don't expect them to act on it... and so on.

Mark Twain, commenting on the inherently futile exercise of trying to teach a pig to fish, observed that "it only serves to annoy the pig and to frighten the fish." So it is with dealing with one type of American as if he or she could become, or act like, another type of American.

In the end (and as a point of reference), if you add up the US population of Students, Caretakers, and Indulgents, the total is 46 percent. That is nearly half the population of the United States and also remarkably near the number of eligible Americans who have failed to vote in the past ten presidential elections!

SOPHISTICATES (10 PERCENT)

Ten percent of our fellow Americans qualify as what we might call Sophisticates. As consumers they are willing to pay the price for better and best, but they are also exceptionally demanding customers. Having paid a premium, they expect premium service.

As citizens, Sophisticates push the envelope of quality in all things. In a very real sense, they concern themselves with supporting the best candidate, identifying the best policies, and generally making the best decisions.

CONVENTIONALS (9 PERCENT)

Sixty years ago, right after the Second World War, the most likely description of the average (i.e., conventional) American might have been someone who had upwardly mobile aspirations, followed the rules, did the right thing, and generally subscribed to an orderly system that required moving through the system on the system's rules. This explains why it was possible for General Motors to create, and for the consuming public to accept, a set of rules for buying cars. According to this now-defunct system, car buyers started out in a Chevrolet, earned their way up to a Pontiac, then advanced to an Oldsmobile. If their economic and life-stage progress allowed, they progressed to a Buick and ultimately acquired a Cadillac.

In all things, including politics, Conventionals are inveterate rule-followers and patient postponers. Since they naturally follow rules, there must be rules to follow. They expect everyone else to follow the same rules, and they are grossly disappointed when they see others breaking the rules.

Expect them to vote in every election because that is the "right thing to do" and to be fully prepared and informed at the ballot box because "that's what you should be." They are more than willing to give the officials they elect an opportunity to prove themselves as "these things take time."

MECHANISTS (17 PERCENT)

If there's one thing for which America justifiably enjoys an international reputation, it is innovation or inventiveness. That comes as no surprise when you consider that nearly one in five Americans qualifies as a Mechanist.

Mechanist consumers get how things work and have the capacity to see how things can be made to work better—usually to their personal or particular advantage. Mechanists are the customers who point out that in your "Buy one, get one free" offer, you failed to be specific about returns. So a Mechanist would like a refund on the paid-for item and would expect to keep the free one, too!

Mechanists have a natural propensity to game the system—any system and every system that can be turned to their advantage. Perhaps that is why the American political system is so fueled by the "one hand washes the other" model. Mechanist constituents will always go to the polls. Count on them in every election. The reason for their presence and participation is their expectation of an appropriate return on their investment. You might say that, right next to the definition of "vested interest" in the dictionary, you would expect to find a picture of the prototypical Mechanist.

STUDENTS (10 PERCENT)

The name of the next group is not meant to imply that they are still in school but that they are perpetual ponderers. Students are those consumers who read every bit of marketing information they can get. In business-to-business situations, these are the prospects who call for second and third meetings for "clarifications" and "responses." In the end, their gratification comes from knowing about your company but not necessarily doing business with it. Student consumers are dangerous for marketers because it is easy to mistake their interest in what you have to say for their intention to ultimately buy what you have to sell.

Students substitute information for action, sort of like the guy who subscribes to *Men's Health* magazine and figures that flipping pages is all the exercise he needs, or the woman who is an avid reader of *Gourmet* magazine or *Architectural Digest* but avoids the kitchen and hasn't actually met with an architect, designer, contractor, or carpenter in her life.

You won't find Students at the voting booth because they're still digesting and evaluating the campaign literature. They know the issues. They just can't get to deciding and acting on them.

CARETAKERS (18 PERCENT)

Caretakers are defined by two imperatives. The first is that they don't feel that they can have any meaningful influence on or control over the things in their lives. The second is an innate understanding that their job on this planet is to leave it neither better nor worse than it was when they got here. In the do-it-yourself business, for example, Caretaker consumers are neither home improvers nor fixer-uppers. They are most likely to be not much more than repairers—and only when inescapably necessary.

Based on the fact that they don't believe they can make a difference anyway, Caretakers see no point in voting.

INDULGENTS (18 PERCENT)

More than one in seven Americans is what we call an Indulgent. Indulgents are people who have some single overriding passion or joy into which they pour every resource—often at the expense of other parts of their lives. A prototypical Indulgent is the guy who owns a thirty-six-foot boat (used) and lives in a 900-square-foot house. Or he might be the blue-collar worker who not only finds the money to buy season tickets to attend every home game of his favorite team but also is likely to attend virtually every game. Indulgent consumers are dangerous for marketers because they often appear more affluent than they are. In our research, Indulgent consumers tended to have a higher percentage of personal aircraft (very, very used and very, very small, of course) and classic cars than their more affluent counterparts.

When it comes to voting, Indulgents generally don't. They are probably at the stadium or polishing their classic car.

GRADUALISTS (10 PERCENT)

One American in ten is a Gradualist. As consumers, Gradualists will do something they decide to do and consider that an end in itself. The last thing a Gradualist consumer expects is to be seen as someone wanting an ongoing relationship of any kind. Frankly, it annoys them. They might come back when and if they need to—but don't count on it! They are not looking for engagement…but they might get there in time.

Gradualist citizens may vote in a particular election for a particular reason, but don't hold your breath waiting for them in the next election. They might even actively volunteer and work in a campaign—once…or at least once in a great while—if they are so moved for a variety of reasons. While they may be occasionally involved, they are decidedly not into commitment.

CHAPTER 35

The 50/50 Divide in Politics

IT SEEMS THAT, NO MATTER WHAT THE ISSUE MAY BE, there is a relatively consistent 50/50 split in America and among Americans across a wide range of issues and questions. In a sense, it is remarkable that we ever achieve anything close to consensus at all.

It is also sobering to appreciate that at least as many Americans support one side of an issue as do the diametrically opposing side and yet we go on as a nation. To me, that means that we need to recognize that the "other side" is big enough so that "they" can't all be extremists and agitators and narrow-minded troublemakers, and neither can "we"—and act accordingly.

I believe that the essential division in America is between Caretakers, Indulgents, and Students (passive cultureographies) on the one hand and Sophisticates, Conventionals, and Mechanists on the other, with Advocates and Gradualists tipping the balance at any moment based on circumstances and how they are affected by a time or situation.

Students tend to "know" more than they act because information substitutes for action. Caretakers don't feel that anything they do really makes a difference so they don't do anything. Indulgents are too busy enjoying what matters most to them.

Mechanists are aware and personally activist, Sophisticates are knowledgeable and engaged, and Conventionals are responsible and motivated. They are, by definition, not only part of the process and the system; they *are* the process and the system.

The tipping points come as a result of the agitation of Advocates and Gradualists, who tip the balance. Recognizing that elections in this country are decided by four or five points of difference and that 8 percent of Americans are Advocates, it is not too difficult to see the equally matched opposing Advocate forces vying to push the scales in their favored direction but also neutralizing each other's efforts. What their activity does is upset the Gradualists among us enough so that they make the final decisions in most elections.

The real power in America is the hands of the Gradualists. Given an adequate impetus of anger or fear or a sense of threat, Gradualists marshal whatever reserves of energy they need to fuel action and take the next necessary and essential step only when it is needed. At what they believe is the inescapable moment to act, they do what they feel impelled to do... and the direction of social or political majority in the country shifts as they exercise their influence. Politically, Gradualists are the proverbial sleeping dogs—benign, invisible, and inconsequential until something stirs them from their slumber. They are the true sleeping giants of the political scene.

Consider how this insight might have affected a string of presidential elections. On the only occasions when a successful presidential candidate received as much as 60% of the vote, a war drove Gradualists to the polls. This was the case of Warren Harding, in the aftermath of the First World War , Franklin Roosevelt's second term which coincided with the threat of war against fascism, Lyndon Johnson's election as the war in Vietnam intensified, and Richard Nixon's second term as the Vietnam war wound down. In fact, Nixon was reelected by more than 10 percentage points over JFK's total popular vote against Nixon. The lowest election margin of the 20th century belonged to Woodrow Wilson in 1912. This was a rare four-way race that included two former presidents (Teddy Roosevelt and William Howard Taft), as well socialist Eugene Debs. Four-term president Franklin Delano Roosevelt got his highest margins during his first terms (57.4% in 1932 and 60.8% in 1936). During the war years, his numbers eroded to 54.7% in 1940 and 53.4% in 1944). While Abraham Lincoln squeaked into office with just under 40% of the popular vote, he was re-elected by 55% of the populace). (See **Table 35-1.**)

Table 35-1. Percentage of Popular Vote Obtained by Each US President from 1824 to 2008					
	Winner	Percentage of Popular Vote		Winner	Percentage of Popular Vote
1824	John Quincy Adams	30.92	1920	Warren G. Harding	60.32
1828	Andrew Jackson	55.93	1924	Calvin Coolidge	54.04
1832	Andrew Jackson	54.74	1928	Herbert Hoover	58.21
1836	Martin Van Buren	50.79	1932	Franklin D. Roosevelt	57.41
1840	William Henry Harrison	52.87	1936	Franklin D. Roosevelt	60.80
1844	James K. Polk	49.54	1940	Franklin D. Roosevelt	54.74
1848	Zachary Taylor	47.28	1944	Franklin D. Roosevelt	53.39
1852	Franklin Pierce	50.83	1948	Harry S. Truman	49.55
1856	James Buchanan	45.29	1952	Dwight D. Eisenhower	55.18
1860	Abraham Lincoln	39.65	1956	Dwight D. Eisenhower	57.37
1864	Abraham Lincoln	55.03	1960	John F. Kennedy	49.72
1868	Ulysses S. Grant	52.66	1964	Lyndon B. Johnson	61.05
1872	Ulysses S. Grant	55.58	1968	Richard Nixon	43.42
1876	Rutherford B. Hayes	47.92	1972	Richard Nixon	60.67
1880	James A. Garfield	48.31	1976	Jimmy Carter	50.08
1884	Grover Cleveland	48.85	1980	Ronald Reagan	50.75
1888	Benjamin Harrison	47.80	1984	Ronald Reagan	58.77
1892	Grover Cleveland	46.02	1988	George H.W. Bush	53.37
1896	William McKinley	51.02	1992	Bill Clinton	43.01
1900	William McKinley	51.64	1996	Bill Clinton	49.23
1904	Theodore Roosevelt	56.42	2000	George W. Bush	47.87
1908	William H. Taft	51.57	2004	George W. Bush	50.73
1912	Woodrow Wilson	41.84	2008	Barack Obama	52.87
1916	Woodrow Wilson	49.24			

CHAPTER 36

The Great American 50/50 Divide

THE FOREGOING DISCUSSION may help to explain how it comes to be that half of America apparently consistently disagrees with the other half—even though the makeup of the halves might be different at different points in time; but disagree we do.

If we are Americans one and all, then why is there such diversity and such diametric division among us? What accounts for the constant shifts in public opinion, and why do we make so much of the latest trends—when we can be pretty sure there's going to be a fairly even split on most things that matter?

The reason we focus so much on how things change over time is because opinion research (invented in the 1930s) is only capable of measuring how the number of people who have an opinion either increases or decreases as a percentage of the population from one period to another. Based on that change-over-time prejudice, we tend to think that any upward or downward shift in a number signals that people are changing their minds about an issue. The idea assumes that, at some point, we all think or thought the same way. Even worse, there is an implied presumption that everyone should share a common baseline from which to deviate.

The following results are less driven by changing standards and opinions over time than they are by the inherent "cultureographic" differences that come to the surface when a particular issue teases them out. The 50 percent conundrum exists because roughly half of Americans are fundamentally different from the other half, cultureographically speaking.

Thinking about this natural American 50/50 divide might be very helpful in appreciating that we are simply not equipped to agree on a great many things. More importantly, it should help us to appreciate that when we are convinced that "they" are wrong, "they" are equally convinced that we are wrong. In the end, when you decide that people who disagree with you are wrong, you are probably wrong at least half of the time.

CHAPTER 37

The Findings: "Fifty Percent of Americans..."

- 50% of Americans oppose stricter gun laws
- 50% of Americans have "very little" or "no" confidence in Congress
- 50% of Americans pay no taxes
- More than 50% of Americans say they are worse off now than they were two years ago
- Fifty-three percent of Americans say Medicare is OK as is or only needs minor change
- 50% of Americans think Iraq had weapons of mass destruction
- Fifty-two percent of Americans say they are unsatisfied with their sex life
- Fifty percent of Americans are satisfied with the cost of their own health care
- Fifty-five percent of Americans believe that housing chickens in cages is not humane
- Fifty-three percent of city dwellers believe global warming is human-caused
- 50% of Americans don't believe in the American Dream
- 50% of Americans support amnesty for illegal immigrants
- Nearly 50% of Americans are anti–free trade
- Nearly half of Americans believe the lottery will provide their retirement nest egg
- Fifty-five percent of Americans are in favor of government regulation of sex, violence, and profanity on television and radio
- 50% of American families have researched their roots

- 50% of Americans believe abortion is morally wrong

- More than 50% of Americans don't know leading hand sanitizers only last two minutes

- 50% of Americans still believe poinsettias are toxic

- 50% of American adults believe abstinence-only education programs are at least somewhat effective in preventing teen pregnancy

- Fifty-four percent of Americans approve of the idea of the Federal Bureau of Investigation (FBI) monitoring the emails of individuals

- 50% of Americans think that giving time to charitable organizations is more important than giving money

- 50% of Americans definitely believe that there is a hell

- Fifty-one percent of Americans oppose drilling for oil in the Arctic National Wildlife Refuge

- 50% of all Americans still lack confidence in the US banking system

CHAPTER 38

The Gen6 Factor— One Really Unprecedented Thing!

I GENERALLY SUBSCRIBE TO THE NOTION that nothing we face is truly unprecedented because things that are "unprecedented" tend to let us off the hook for trying to manage them. On one score, I have to accept the truly unprecedented as a fait accompli. This is the Gen6 Factor—the fact that, for the first time in recorded human history, there are six living and vital generations of Americans competing in the marketplace, deploying their political power, and exerting their will and their considerable economic resources in many different facets of our lives.

Each of the six American generations experiences the same reality—

for example, something as fundamental as work, or the home, or the automobile—yet each has a fundamentally different appreciation of what that reality is. These experiences are evaluated by different micro values systems. They are understood using different generational lexicons and generation-specific change vectors.

When you analyze the attitudes and behaviors of all six generations, what becomes apparent is not only that they are different, but that in a very real sense these characteristics are also cyclical. Understanding future generations and how they will approach things is a great deal easier if you see the link between any current generation and its appropriate predecessor generation. To fully understand Millennials, for example, you need to develop a deep appreciation of the GI Generation. In a sense, they are the same generation but evolving under very different circumstances. The same can be said for every American generation. What appear to be unique generational markers are actually echoes of a specific predecessor generation.

The generational conversation makes sense in the context of the America Code because we need to see the code for what it is—an underlying constant regardless of the generation at bat in any given moment of our history. In every generation, disenfranchised diligent optimists will stir the pot and add fuel to the American dynamic—although the way they go about expressing it may differ somewhat from generation to generation. Americans will continue to be congenitally addicted to independence and suffer from collective amnesia. In short, all of the America Code will continue to ground each generation. There is value in appreciating the constancy while accepting the variations of the moment.

At the same time, as we will see in this section, the generational wheel actually goes round and round rather than on and on. Each generation is not completely different from all the generations that preceded it. Each generation is, in fact, the counterpart of a specific prior generation, an observation that goes a long way toward explaining why Archetypal Americans in the 1700s were a lot like the Archetypal Americans of the current millennium.

CHAPTER 39

American Generations by the Numbers

FOR THE FIRST TIME IN HUMAN HISTORY, we have managed to have six contemporaneous generations of Americans living in the country. These generations are defined by the social scientists who do the demographic heavy lifting.

The process is too lengthy to discuss here, but it is based in part on formative events that create a clear line of distinction between one generation and the next. Each group of birth babies ends up with a generational label that derives either from the things that happen to them at the time of their formative years or from the things they end up doing in those formative years.

For example, the Boomer generation was easy enough to name since it consists of the children of the postwar boom in births after World War II. The GI generation was also easy enough to designate, as they were the generation that qualified to soldier during the war.

The labels used here are borrowed from the 1991 book *Generations: The History of America's Future 1534 to 2069,* by Neil Howe and William Strauss, and their 2000 book *Millennials Rising: The Next Great Generation.* Each of these generations has also been described by other names—for example, Generation X has been called Baby Busters and Generation 13 while Millennials have been labeled Generation Y. I particularly favor calling my children's generation Millennials rather than Generation Y because it seems a bit like courting fate if we begin the generational nomenclature at the end of the alphabet. After *X* and *Y* there is only one designator left, and I'm not sure I want go down that road with its potential implications.

As a point of reference, the chart below describes the birth years assigned to each of these six generations as well as its age range in 2010 and the original size of each American generation making up the Gen6 (see **Table 39-1**).

Table 39-1. Gen 6 Makeup			
Generation	Birth Years	2012 Age	Generation Size
GI	1901–1924	86–109	56.6 million
Silent	1925–1942	68–85	52.5 million
Boomer	1943–1960	50–67	78.2 million
Gen-X	1961–1981	29–49	69.5 million
Millennial	1982–2001	9–28	100 million
Homeland	2002–2022	8– (–12)	TBD

Generational breaks from William Strauss and Neil Howe, *Generations: The History of America's Future, 1584–2069* (William Morrow, 1991) and *Millennials Rising* (Vintage Books, 2000). Generational size from National Center for Health Statistics/US CDC

Two things are made obvious by this chart. The first is that not every generation covers exactly the same age range (the birth years of a typical generation will fall somewhere around twenty years). GIs, for example, were born between 1901 and 1924—a period of twenty-three years. On the other hand, the birth years for Silents are 1925 to 1942—a period of seventeen years. Boomers came into the world between 1943 and 1960, another seventeen-year generation, while Generation X was birthed in a neat score years between 1961 and 1981.

The graph below compares the historical and current numbers for the six generations (see **Figure 39-1**).

If historical precedents mean anything, we can expect the Homeland generation to be smaller in total number than Millennials. This proposition makes sense when you consider the fact that Millennials are waiting for later marriages. Moreover, according to the 2010 Census, Millennial women have a significantly lower birthrate than did their Generation X counterparts and more than one-third of married Millennial couples do not have children.

Historical and Current Populations
of the Six Generations

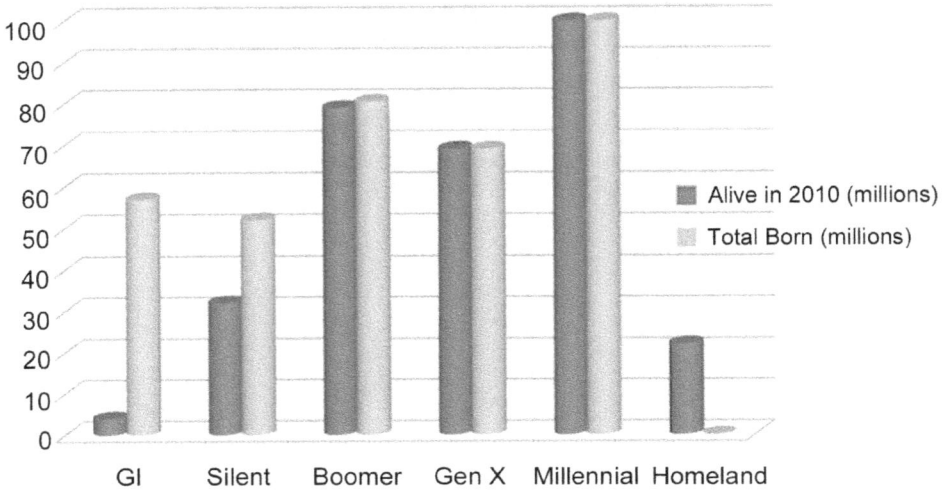

Figure 39-1. Historical versus current numbers of the six generations.

CHAPTER 40

What Matters Most about Generations:
Numbers and Dollars

WHEN IT COMES TO GENERATIONS, two dimensions really matter: the total population and the economics as expressed in buying power. As to the impact of generational size, consider this: the Silents followed the GIs (the "greatest generation," according to Tom Brokaw) and preceded the Baby Boomers (the largest generation ever...at that time). Sandwiched between two overperforming generations, it is no wonder that they were called "Silents"!

What the simple reality of explosive growth on the part of the Boomers did to America was that it created an expectation of boom, of growth, of ever-increasing scale and unlimited horizons ahead. That expectation of "more" fueled much of our postwar recovery and drove America to be greater, better, bigger, grander.

Then a demographic revisionism intruded in the form of Generation X. If every Boomer was driven by "more is more" and if competition for jobs (there were more Boomers than jobs) drove them to create new opportunities, Generation X put on the brakes and moved us into a kind of expectation and entitlement based on the numbers.

Members of Generation X have a reputation for being lazy, unambitious, demanding, disloyal—well, it's a long list, and much of it is not flattering. But the fact is Gen-X's birth babies are victims of the math. They represented an entry-level workforce considerably smaller than its forebear generation of Boomers. That meant Gen-Xers had more opportunities than they knew what to do with. Some say they didn't do much with the choices.

That kind of choice breeds selectivity. It also increases the probability of shifting from one job to another pretty much at will. The other thing that this much-smaller-than-anticipated generation did was confound the Boomer-driven American marketing engine. Based on the Boomers, our expectations were for more and more. Growth in all its many forms had become the natural presumption of American business. It is, in the end, difficult to sustain growth when the number of people required to make that happen is suddenly much smaller.

Let's take a look at the size of the six existing American generations. As it happens, each of them is still big enough to survive as its own country. There are already enough Homelands to populate Australia (population 22 million), and they already control a spending power equal to the gross domestic product of Hungary ($150 billion). We are still adding new members to the Homeland generation at the rate of 460 every hour.

Every Millennial that is ever going to be, already is. The final count comes in at roughly 100 million. That clearly makes the generation significantly larger than the Boomers (by some 20 million) and almost as large as the population of Mexico. While by no means at the peak of their spending years, Millennials currently match the Czech Republic in spending power ($200 billion).

Members of Generation X number roughly 70 million—a bit bigger than the population of France. They also account for some $800 billion in spending power, or approximately the gross domestic product of The Netherlands.

One unprecedented result of the Gen6 Factor is that, as life expectancies get longer, so does vitality...in every sense of the word. Consequently, Millennials and Homelands are the first generation in history to be parented by two generations of parents: Gen-Xers and Boomers. In the case of Boomer parents, the younger children can be either delayed first children or second families. Because this simple fact breaks the historical, three-generational "my parents, myself, my child" pattern and turns people who "should" be grandparents into the parents of even very young children, it will affect the family dynamic in many ways for years to come.

Boomers are still the premier American generation in terms of spending power, accounting for $2.2 *trillion* in spending (roughly the entire economy of the United Kingdom). At 78 million strong, Boomers could be a nation the size of Germany.

One interesting statistic relevant to Silents (the next-to-oldest generation) is this: of all the people in the history of the world who have ever achieved the age of 65, half are alive today. This is what makes it possible for America's Silent generation of 32 million to represent a viable economy equal to Poland's (at $800 billion) and numerous enough to almost populate Canada.

Finally, there are the GIs. The generation that fought World War II is still fighting gravity and aging. While their numbers have come down significantly from a peak of 57 million, don't go counting them out of anything. The surviving 3 million GIs today still control a spending power equal to that of the Republic of Vietnam (some $100 billion) and, if transplanted as a group, could take over Albania from its 3 million current citizens—not that they ever would, of course.

CHAPTER 41

Generational Micro Values Systems

ONE OF THE BENEFITS of the cultureographic research model we talked about earlier in this book is identifying and dimensionalizing micro values systems—the ways groups of people interpret and value a particular thing compared to other groups.

As it happens, looking at micro values systems is another way to add depth to understanding generational nuances around the things on which we spend a lot of time, energy, and money—some basic Americanisms, if you will—like education, work, home, fun, and the automobile. Knowing that will further an appreciation of why Americans often look at the same thing, but clearly see something else depending on the lens through which we see it.

Cultureographic mapping was originally developed to improve marketing (it was successful, for example, in increasing direct response advertising rates by as much as 500 percent), but the principles that came from polling more than 35,000 Americans apply to universal decision-making processes and can help us better understand what the "generational thing" is all about. Let's look at the first three universal aspirations— Education, Work, and Home (see **Table 41-1**).

Table 41-1. Gen6 — Education, Work, and Home			
Generation	**Education**	**Work**	**Home**
GI	Dream	Labor	Rent
Silent	Privilege	Duty	Own
Boomer	Birthright	Fulfillment	Invest
Gen-X	Means	Necessity	Use
Millennial	Job	Learning	Guest
Homeland	Life	Deliverables	Option to Buy

From William Strauss and Neil Howe, *Generations: The History of America's Future, 1584–2069* (William Morrow, 1991) and *Millennials Rising* (Vintage Books, 2000).

CHAPTER 42

Generational Perspectives on Education in America

EVEN THOUGH ONLY ABOUT 27 PERCENT OF AMERICANS have gone on to education beyond high school, the importance of education is at the core of who we are as a nation and as a people. There is, and has always been, the assumption of a connection between getting a better education and improving your circumstances. Historically, education (whether that be public education at the high school level or beyond) has been the great American leveler that makes it possible for so many of us to "rise above" whatever circumstances in which we find ourselves. It is education that gives an immigrant with no foundation in this country the platform to succeed and successfully compete with more established citizens.

That universal point of view on education looks decidedly different when seen through the lens of each American generation.

For the GIs, education was the virtually impossible dream— something to which you were neither entitled nor encouraged. A perfectly understandable perspective in a generation where many children started working right after high school or even earlier so as to contribute their small paychecks to the family income pool. Even though many GIs did avail themselves of the GI Bill and its educational entitlements, their number was a small minority, as you would expect of a generation that did not grow up believing in this possibility.

Silents, having seen the postwar boom of GI benefit scholarships and loans earned by their parents' generation, understood education to be an attainable goal available to anyone worthy enough and responsible enough to make the most of such an opportunity and to work at earning the opportunity. For Silents, an advanced education, if it were your great luck to have it, carried with it the charge to make the most of it and be worthy.

By the time Boomers got close to college age, the view was that a college education was a kind of expected birthright. Most Boomers felt it was their due to go to college, along with their right to a government loan or grant with which to pay for that education and the possibility that they may or may not actually repay the loan.

Gen-Xers were the generation that reformed the idea of education from something of value in its own right into a kind of technical training for work life. The purpose of a Gen-Xer education was less about developing the individual to become all he or she could be and more about providing specific job-related skills. It was at this point that the idea of a liberal arts education in America first began to be considered "old-fashioned" and impractical.

I have to admit to a prejudice on this point as, having been the beneficiary of a Jesuit educational system and having seen its impact on my own life and on those of others, I see the practical side of the classical approach. The fundamental Jesuit theory is twofold: (a) As a young person you don't know enough to make good choices about what you should learn, and in the end, "soft" studies such as history, philosophy, and literature prove to have practical value over time; and (b) The important thing is to learn how to learn and how to think. Given the incredible rate of change in the world today and the fact that most people will have multiple careers over their lifetimes, it would seem that such basic skills will prove more valuable than the knowledge of specific content.

Having been told from their earliest days that their number one job was to get a good education, Millennials have made a natural connection that learning is work. In fact, for them, it cuts both ways: If learning is a job, then a job should be learning. Most managers seem not to have noticed that Millennial employees are best motivated when they continue to feel that they are learning something and most likely to bail when that ceases to be the case. (Word of advice to American management: It is better to mentor Millennials than to manage them.)

There hasn't been enough time yet for the Homeland generation to develop a point of view on education, but it is likely to be the acquisition, decoding, and deployment of information. Handling access to and managing the bulk of information rather than honing insight and perspective seem to be the increasing focus of education. At the same time, every moment in the life of a Homeland is a moment of learning because there's always something new to find out about since new possibilities are being created or presented by the second in their world. For them, life, education, learning will be fully interchangeable, seamless, and fluid.

CHAPTER 43

Generational Perspectives on Work in America

WORK IS THE NEXT GREAT AMERICAN FUNDAMENTALISM. For GIs, work was understood to be something hard—something you were not expected to enjoy nor from which it was necessary for you to derive much satisfaction. That's what retirement is for—the day when you stop doing something you either hate or dislike and begin to do what you really love for the rest of the "golden years" of your life.

Silents view work as another demand for responsibility and duty. Whatever place or role or job you have in life, you need to earn your keep, to be worthy of the opportunity.

Boomers view work as a source of personal fulfillment. If a job isn't fulfilling, you go get another job. If that one ranks low on the fulfillment scale, go get another. A personal quest for professional fulfillment is the explanation behind the lengthy and varied job histories of many Boomers.

Gen-Xers view work as a necessity. Work is what you do to get money. Money is what you need so that you can enjoy life. Enjoyment is the ultimate goal of making a living; work is not the end in itself.

As we said earlier, Millennials don't see a dividing line between job and learning. Learning is your first job and every job had better offer some form of learning because Millennials need to feel they are growing in development in their job.

I have had personal experience with young people working in high-tech systems sales. Many of them earn a quarter to half a million dollars from their sales positions. However, after a few months, many of them desperately want to get into management positions, not because they are looking for the power or the perks but because they feel they have learned everything learnable in their current jobs. More often than not, such a switch actually will decrease their income. That is not the point, since a lower income is clearly an acceptable price for a new set of learnings.

Homelands will not think of work as a place to report. I see their workplace as wherever they might be and they are less likely to be defined by job titles than they will be by deliverables. In a future (think next decade) when jobs will disappear, be redefined, and reinvented continually, Homeland workers will be defined by what they output—in a kind of return to the old model of "piecework." In that way, the Homeland workforce will be able to adapt to creating what is needed more readily and more naturally than prior generations.

CHAPTER 44

Generational Perspectives on the Home in America

HOME OWNERSHIP IS A CENTRAL THEME IN AMERICA. It is also the prime driver of the American consumer experience because a home is a place you need to fill with "stuff"—and stuff is what consumerism is all about. There is also something in the American genetic code that wants its little piece of territory and its little roof. Given the fact that most of America wandered across the Atlantic from a Europe where it was impossible for the average person to own anything, this should not be surprising—so the home and the American character are inextricably intertwined.

The GI generation was not as connected to the idea of owning a home as we are today. They didn't expect to have one largely because of the pain and aftermath of the Great Depression, but also because homes were simply unaffordable for the vast majority of Americans. The GI view was that what you were was a renter—a kind of twentieth-century sharecropper. An owner is what you may have aspired to be. That is the great theme of Frank

Capra's classic movie *It's a Wonderful Life,* starring James Stewart. In the movie the whole purpose of the Bailey Brothers Savings & Loan was to move renters out of the grubby, exploitative clutches of Old Man Potter into their own affordable, modest homes.

By the time Silents came of age, the prospect of owning a home had been significantly improved by the GI Bill of Rights and by America's postwar invention of "ticky-tacky" houses in massive developments, beginning with Long Island's Levittown. As home ownership became an increasingly achievable status, Silents insisted on full ownership as soon as possible. The goal of paying off the mortgage and having a mortgage-burning party drove them to be diligent loan repayers.

Boomers took the concept of owning a home to an entirely new plane—home and hearth as investment. As Boomers approached the purchase of their first and subsequent homes, their prime consideration was prospective resale value. Boomer intentions were never to remain in the first home until retirement. In fact, the home was supposed to provide for that retirement by increasing in value and creating equity that would ultimately be cashed out. This system worked well for a while and well enough for some of Boomers, particularly if they did the work themselves and kept an eye on the difference between what they put into the home and what that investment would generate at the time of sale. Those were the good old days indeed.

For Gen-Xers, the home is a thing to be used. It doesn't need to belong to you. It is a platform and a support system for your life. If Boomers contributed to creating the great Do-It-Yourself Movement and focused on home improvement, Gen-Xers have been at the forefront of home repurposing—making the home suitable to support and enhance the lives owners lead.

While most American Millennials aren't quite yet at the home-buying stage of their lives, the way they view the home is already discernible. For a Millennial, the home is a place where you are the visiting guest. One of the first shocks to Millennials who move out of the nest (mostly to dorms and apartments) is that toilet paper does not magically appear on the holder and that pantries are not stocked by elves in the middle of the night. It is this discomfiting insight that has brought so many Millennials back home after a brief excursion out in the real world. It also helps to explain why the new order of things at universities is the five-year or six-year undergraduate plan.

Homelands are a long way from making their first home acquisition, but it is likely that they will view their homes as tools. A tool is defined as something that helps you do the work you want to do. That is exactly what the Homelands' homes of the future will be. That being said, they will want to try those tools on for "fit" — recognizing intuitively that every major decision needs to be tested on an ongoing basis. Home sellers and realtors will be wise to consider that Homeland generation members are going to be less likely to fully commit to a home purchase until they have had adequate time to assess the way in which that home will support their evolving and fluid lifestyles.

CHAPTER 45

Fun and the Automobile in America

NO CONVERSATION ABOUT AMERICAN VALUES, or generational values, or anything about America would be complete without the two basic Americanisms for which we are best known and which have contributed most to the way we exert influence on the rest of the world.

In some ways, these might be considered the essence of the American personality that we radiate: We LOVE to have fun. We LOVE our cars! (See **Table 45-1**.)

Table 45-1. Gen 6 Fun and Cars		
Generation	**Fun**	**Automobile**
GI	Release	Indulgence
Silent	Reward	Rite of Passage
Boomer	2nd Job	Achievement
Gen-X	Assumption	Utility Vehicle
Millennial	Norm	Passenger Space
Homeland	The Process	Service

From William Strauss and Neil Howe, *Generations: The History of America's Future, 1584–2069* (William Morrow, 1991) and *Millennials Rising* (Vintage Books, 2000).

CHAPTER 46

Generational Perspectives on Fun in America

As WE SAID EARLIER, the "pursuit of happiness" is one of the great driving forces for Americans. While "fun" is an American universal, the form it takes varies greatly from generation to generation. No country on the face of the earth is as obsessed with and fixated upon having fun.

For the GI generaton, fun was literally a release of pent-up emotions. A generally reserved generation like the GIs needed some way to blow off steam regularly. One unstated mantra of the generation: "Work like a dog Monday through Friday—get drunk Saturday night."

The Silent generation tweaked this concept into an endless parade of sufferings and rewards. In their view, you couldn't expect a reward like fun until you first endured some suffering—like work. Suffer/Reward/Suffer was their rallying call. That is why Silents made the ideal prototypical consumer. They put up with all manner of obstacles and impediments to get to the rewards at the end of the rainbow. One of the best things that ever happened to Silents was the introduction of the layaway plan, which allowed you to fixate on an object of your desire, then claim it, only to put yourself through the suffering of earning it before you could possess it.

Boomers, in contrast, believed that fun is something you need to take very very seriously. If Boomers fail to come back from a vacation at least as tired as when they left, then it couldn't have been very much fun. In fact, Boomers believe in competitive fun. My fun needs to be better, grander, and more exhausting than your fun. My vacation needs to be better than yours.

In the Gen-Xer world, things are "supposed" to be fun. Gen-Xers have a high "fun" expectation from everything they do…including on the job. When they realize that something has ceased to be fun, they immediately look for someone to take note and to correct this egregious imbalance in their favor. Gen-Xers are not happy if they are not having fun at what they do.

Millennials, given their virtually bottomless fountain of choices and technologically supported access to alternatives, have developed a finely tuned, ultrasensitive, un-fun early warning system. Unlike the Gen-Xers, who are conscious of the transition from fun to un-fun, Millennials will cease an activity long before it ever actually makes them consciously feel things have changed for the worse. It all comes together naturally for them in the low-tech television channel changer—or as they see it, their electronic experience surfboard.

To really understand this phenomenon, put a Boomer in a room with a Millennial and a TV set. Give the Millennial the "clicker" and watch the fun. The Millennial effortlessly moves from channel to channel in nanoseconds because he immediately perceives the probability that something will not be fun enough to hold his attention so he instantly makes a change. The befuddled and confused Boomer, trying to keep up, will invariably be uncomfortable with the choices because she needs more time to make any such determination. She also can't press that button anywhere near as fast.

Marshall McLuhan, the Canadian sage on society and the media of the 1970s, made famous the statement "the medium is the message." By which he meant that the way in which we disseminated information would trump the value of the information itself. I, for one, believe MM was wrong. His way of thinking, however, applies to understanding how the Homelands are redefining "fun." Since Homelands enjoy unprecedented choice and an intense (although probably exaggerated) sense of control over everything in their lives, the act of processing possibilities so as to transform them into decisions and outcomes, the joy comes from the journey rather than from the destination. Any particular outcome will matter less than the route through which it was created.

CHAPTER 47

Generational Perspectives on the Automobile in America

ONE OF THE FIRST THINGS that many visitors to this country immediately notice is the ubiquitous presence of personal automobiles. My aunt, visiting from Poland, once said to me, "So many rich people in America. Everybody has a car!" Cars and the roads they require certainly contributed to the industrialization of this country. But, truly, there is a special, highly personal relationship between Americans and their automobiles. This, too, is affected by generational micro values systems.

Much as in the case of the home, the members of the GI generation got through most of their lives without having a personal automobile—and certainly not a new one. In spite of Mr. Ford's wonderful assembly line and "reasonable" prices, cars were less than essential for the GIs. In the first place, you could walk to most places you needed to get to. Theirs was an America in which every neighborhood had an easily accessible source of food and services within easy walking distance. The "corner store" really was on a corner down the street. The "local butcher" was so local you could walk there and walk home with all the ground beef you needed. It wasn't until America was *malled* in the 1950s that driving to shop became the norm.

For Silents, the automobile took on a different value. It became a sort of rite of passage, with automotive ownership milestones marking the progress from one socioeconomic status to another. Chevys were cars for society's beginners, who then made upwardly mobile progress through Pontiacs, Oldsmobiles, Buicks, and culminated at the stratospheric heights of achievement represented by the Cadillac.

Boomers had little patience for such a process and were far more interested in the automotive badge of the moment than the steps required to merit it. Can you say "Beamer, NOW?" If leasing got you there faster, so much the better.

Gen-Xers were the first to think of the automobile as a "utility vehicle"—not in the *Car and Driver* magazine sense of "SUV," but with the understanding that a car is something that serves a purpose in your life. It doesn't have to belong to you—it could be somebody else's car—all you're looking for is the use of it. Sometimes it will be a truck; at other times it will be a convertible. Gen-Xers' freewheeling approach to things automotive made them less attached to any one car and more accessible to the collective "car pool" concept.

The one fascinating thing about Millennials and automobiles, even in car-crazy America, is that Millennials appear to be the generation most likely to procrastinate about getting that driver's license. I have never seen so many sixteen-year-olds so remarkably uninterested in driving. The reason is simple. Millennials have spent more time than any prior generation in the backseat being chauffeured to *their* destinations by their parents. If there is such a thing as a "soccer mom," it is only because there are teams of soccer Millennials, and hockey Millennials, and karate lesson Millennials, and so on. This is one generation that has figured out that owning a car brings with it a whole series of undesirable consequences—parking, fueling, maintenance, and insurance—while all they really need is a ride OMG!

Where the Homelands will take the American automotive experience is still anybody's guess. However, all things considered, it would be a good bet that the ideal car for Homelands will be one they can use at will. They may well transform the idea of automobile ownership into automobile access. Some smart marketer should begin looking into a new kind of "automobile club"—one in which you pay a monthly fee and have access to a car wherever and whenever you actually need one—all gassed, all insured, and even pre-parked. As a good futurist, I foresaw this direction years ago when the number of "off-lease" vehicles began to create burgeoning fleets of cars that were neither used in the classic sense, nor new, nor ever actually owned by any one person. As a poor investor, I did nothing with the insight. But a company named Zipcar has come close to monetizing the vision. Simply put, for Homelands, an automobile is more likely to be thought of as a service than as a product.

CHAPTER 48

Every Generation Can't Be Worse than the One That Preceded It!

Why can't they be like we were, perfect in every way?
Oh, what's the matter with kids today?

Bye Bye Birdie, *the musical, 1960*

WHEN IT COMES TO THE MOMENT OF PASSING THE TORCH to the next generation, each currently ascendant generation is unequivocally convinced that their successors are also their lessers. There exists an ongoing feeling that the new generation just isn't quite as good as the current generation.

There are two problems with this first-is-best/last-is-worst approach to things. The first is a simple reality check. Let's just jump back to 8,000 BC as a reasonable starting point for human social evolution, as archaeologists have some general agreement that it was this long ago that the biblical city of Jericho was settled.[16]

That means, over some 10,000 years, we would have had roughly 500 generations. If we accept the idea that each generation is progressively worse than its predecessor, then either the current generational crop must be beyond abysmal or the first generation kicked off human progress at such a high level that we really got a good start and may still have another 500 generations before things get really out of hand.

The second problem is that the complaint of "why can't they be like we were, perfect in every way" has been a recurring theme for thousands of years. For example, around 400 BC the ancient Greek playwright Aristophanes wrote in *The Clouds,*

The children now love luxury; they show disrespect for elders and love chatter in place of exercise. Children are tyrants, not servants of the households. They no longer rise when their elders enter the room. They contradict their parents, chatter before company, gobble up dainties at the table, cross their legs, and tyrannize over their teachers.

(This quotation is sometimes attributed to Socrates.)

If that isn't ironic enough, here's a quote from the Greek poet Hesiod, writing some 400 years earlier:

> *I see no hope for the future of our people if they are dependent on the frivolous youth of today, for certainly all youth are reckless beyond words. When I was a boy, we were taught to be discreet and respectful of elders, but the present youth are exceedingly wise [as in "smart-mouthed"] and impatient of restraint.*

Hesiod was concerned about the generations of Greeks who were about four hundred years away from creating what is generally agreed to have been the "Golden Age" of Greece.

So if the alpha and omega model (first and last) of successively worse generations doesn't work, what does?

In their terrific book *Generations: The History of America's Future, 1584 to 2069* (1991), authors Neil Howe and William Strauss have come up with an interesting and I believe accurate alternative model. They went back in history in England and tracked twenty-five generations right up to the current Homelands.

After poring through every available fact about each of these one score and five generations, they created a model that provides a fascinating picture of what happens in generational succession. According to the fundamental finding of the book, there are only four generational types (Prophet/Idealist, Nomad/Reactive, Hero/Civic, and Artist/Adaptive) that succeed each other in an almost unbroken chain back to their earliest documentable generation. I urge very serious readers to tackle the 500-some pages of this wonderful book wherever they can find a copy.

The basic theory (which I view as intuitively correct) says that today's Homeland generation has all the markings and dispositions of its Silent counterparts. That means GIs and Millennials are the same (only different), Gen-Xers pair up with the "Lost Generation" of the 1880s, and Boomers line up with the "Missionary Generation" of the 1860s.

If we look at the connection between Millennials and GIs, some things do make a lot more sense. GIs came of age during the Great Depression, when they learned to buy only the things they really needed. Millennials are coming of age during a parallel period of economic instability. While they have resources, they are also careful about how they spend their money. With virtually limitless possibilities available to them, Millennials turn out to be "strategic shoppers"—they will pay whatever it takes to buy the things that really matter most to them, on the one hand, and "make do" when it comes to less important things.

This helps to explain why it is possible for a young person in a first job to fork over $800 for an iPad (which really, really matters) and then make up for splurging by shopping for less important items at extreme discount or even secondhand clothing stores (which explains the growing trend toward "after-market fashion").

It takes roughly four generations to complete a cycle. That means today's Millennials are a virtual counterpart to the values and attitudes (only expressed in a contemporary fashion) of the GI generation. To get a handle on where the Homeland generation is headed, what you need to do is go into a solid analysis of the Silent generation. In this way, it is both easier and more comforting to understand that each new generation is *not* unprecedented at all—so long as you factor in the current circumstances.

CHAPTER 49

Generations and Technology

MUCH IS MADE OF "TECHNOLOGY" THESE DAYS. Technology is doing this to our lives. Technology is changing that in society. Because of technology, our lives will never be the same again...and so on. It's almost as if we, in the first half of the twenty-first century, have the audacity to be taking credit for the invention of technology and for being the first to experience technologically driven change. Either we have stopped teaching history, or we have forgotten how to appreciate its lessons (I know, Santayana again!).

Point: When the first fellow figured out how to attach a rock to the end of a stick, that technological breakthrough changed his world forever, and the world of everyone around him. He immediately went from being the weakling in the tribe to its most dangerous member. The technological advancement of the club was very good for the inventor, but not so good for anyone who crossed his path—a decided game-changer, that one.

Then there's the technology that can put into your hands the sum of human knowledge. Give you completely portable, fully interactive access to every answer imaginable—and make it something you could hold in the palm of your hand. Always on. Always ready. Always able to expand your knowledge or unleash your imagination. Something almost anyone could have anywhere in the world. This is one technology that requires neither some assembly nor batteries. It's the book and it's been completely changing our lives (especially the Bible) ever since it was invented more than 500 years ago.

OK, more recently: Which US president was the first to wage war involving electronic communications and high-tech troop deployment? Bush I? Clinton? Bush II? Carter?

Actually, it was Abraham Lincoln. Lincoln figured out that the telegraph let him be in touch with "feet on the ground" in the battlefield. It made it possible for him to know what was happening in the field faster than the generals commanding the battles. At the same time, another technological breakthrough made it possible for Lincoln to act on timely information. He could ship needed equipment of manpower immediately where it was most needed—"immediately" being a relative term of the times, as Lincoln could load up his trains and get 25,000 men to the front in a matter of days while General Lee's troops, using the same transport of feet and hooves as Alexander the Great, would take weeks to get to the same place.

Certainly, the Confederates also had rail transport. In fact, Confederate infantry reinforcements under the command of General Joe Johnston arrived by train and helped save the day for the Confederates at the First Battle of Bull Run (Manassas). The fact remains, however, that the North enjoyed a far superior and far more extensive rail system and used that system more effectively and frequently than the South.

Technology is a constant of the human condition, and the cycle of higher-level technology supplanting earlier technology is a continual norm. What is different is the technological evolutionary context. In other words, the physical nature and capabilities of technology change. The idea of television, of transmitting visual signals over a long distance, is actually quite old. Television as we know it had to wait for the invention of the radio and the vacuum tube.

And that is where the America Code comes into play. As a nation, we have probably pushed the boundaries of technological evolution farther than other countries. Tinkering and experimentation are part and parcel of being American, beginning with the invention of an entirely new political system.

As a result, the things that are inevitable, the appearance, growth, decline, and replacement of pretty much everything, now occurs in an environment where the possibilities increase at a dramatic rate. We feel overwhelmed by the pace and degree of change because we keep increasing the possibilities for that change. In America, over the past few generations, technology has done the same thing to and for each generation. It has changed the game, broken old rules, and created new ones. Each American generation has its own defining moment of technology.

The GI generation came of age at a time of two great technological changes in the world. One would transform not only transportation but also society, and the other was the first instance of high-tech electronic social networking. Henry Ford's magic assembly line took in steel, rubber, canvas, and wood at one end and spit out social change machines by the thousands at the other. The Model T made America's GI generation the first truly mobile group of people in history. Not only could America's citizenry go out for a weekend jaunt in the old jalopy, but they could also pick up and move across the country—wherever jobs, opportunities, or the simple call of the next new thing or the next new place might take them.

Besides opening up America in a whole new way, the Model T also created legions of mechanically inclined tinkerers. While the venerable black "T" (there is some question whether the *T* stands for "touring [car]" or whether successfully building it ate up the first nineteen letters of the alphabet in prototypes) was a dependable car, it also required owners who were comfortable enough to do their own servicing and repairs.

As a historical side note, these masses of natural-born, Ford-inspired tinkerers had a real advantage on the twentieth-century battlefield where technologically advanced engines of war needed as much care and attention as America's early automobiles.

The second great technological revolution that defined America's GI generation was the invention and relative popularity of electronic social networking (although on a smaller scale than today's version) in the form of amateur (or "ham") radio. For a relatively small investment and some basic smarts and instructions, thousands of enterprising Americans (and others around the world) created a global network of amateur radio transmitting and receiving stations. As a kind of foreshadowing of what is happening in the first part of the twenty-first century, these radio enthusiasts quickly formed national and international communities based on their ability to instantly communicate with one another and to cross international borders and time zones. Global electronic intimacy had its roots in the ham radio movement.

America's Silent generation saw the world shrink even smaller with their version of unprecedented technological breakthroughs. Lowell Thomas (an early radio commentator and host) and his contemporaries connected everyday Americans to events and experiences around the world. Radio created a sense of intimate community across America—including Franklin Delano Roosevelt's reassuring post-Depression "fireside chats" when an American president literally visited America's living rooms in time of crisis.

One other earth-shrinking technology of the 1930s came in the form of Pan American's China Clippers. The Clippers were large "flying boats" that could take off and land on water. This technology turned what had been a six-day cruise from San Francisco to Hawaii into a short seventeen-hour flight. The lavish accommodations and unprecedented speeds made it possible for business travelers to get as far as China, some 10,000 miles away, for business trips of reasonable duration.

Boomers' technological defining moment came in the 1960s, exemplified by General Electric's "Carousel of Progress" at the 1965 World's Fair in New York. Along with the exhibit's unforgettable theme song ("There's a great big beautiful tomorrow waiting at the end of every day"), young Boomers were impressed by the promise of an unending parade of regulated, corporately generated technological progress ahead.

Boomers were also the first to cut the cord—the telephone cord, that is. In 1973, the first cellular telephone call was made by a Motorola engineer using a Motorola Dyna TAC telephone while walking the streets of New York. His first call? A pernicious call to Motorola's rival AT&T Bell Labs, just to rub it in. When released for full popular consumption ten years later in 1983, the Dyna TAC was over a foot long and nearly four inches thick. It weighed in at nearly two pounds.

Gen-Xers' principal defining technology included the first recorded instances of time travel. OK, not exactly time travel, but time-shifting in the form of video recorders. The devices freed the average television viewer from network schedules and real-time viewing to time-shift viewing. With its general availability (in the VHS format that eventually outmarketed Sony's original Beta of the 1970s) in the late 1980s, this simple device made it possible to control time. No longer did audiences need to choose between one program and another airing at the same time. They could now have it all. The implications for social change are significant when a group of people become first comfortable and then insistent on realigning the reality they experience—particularly when they are given the tools to make it so.

The ubiquitous and common use of cell phones also created the first "disconnected-yet-more-connected" American generation. Freed from wires and now on "all air" communications, Millennials literally redefined the idea of "connected." What was once a concept defined by copper wire and centralization has for them become a continually plugged-in connectivity anywhere, any time, by any number of means—except wires.

The developing theme of transformation rose to new heights with the Millennials. On the one hand, this generation has grown up with incredible technological advancement. On the other hand, such accelerated high-tech solutioning is both normal and expected by Millennials. In fact, their expectations rise ever higher with each succeeding technological development. Millennials are the first market segment for which it is consistently impossible to exceed any expectations.

The real defining technological moment for Millennials was not even in the realm of the real technological boom happening all around them, however, but in the world of make-believe. In the 1980s, an entertainment juggernaut and a social force for change coalesced in the form of *The Transformers*. What began as a kind of shticky television program eventuated into a Millennial moment of major proportions.

What *The Transformers* taught America's Millennials is that, through technology, you can transform the reality that either bores or disinterests you into the reality that is ideal for you...for the moment. The underlying message of the Transformers (robots both good and bad that can transmogrify themselves into other forms of technology such as cars, planes, and even animal-like mecho-creatures) is that if something doesn't suit you, you can change it into something that does.

That is one reason why Millennials are so into skins for their electronic devices and why Google alone lets you make it your own through more than 35,000 Persona designs. Every generation from Boomer back would be overwhelmed by such choices and at a loss to understand any rational justification for their existence in the first place. Millennials can't get enough of personal transformation.

In spite of the fact that the oldest Homelands are somewhere around ten years of age, it isn't too difficult to see the connection between their generation and technology—and where it's likely to go. If Gen-Xers naturally gravitated to control of time and Millennials to transformation, Homelands are likely to push to new boundaries in what will at that point be the ultimate technological convergence.

We are already beginning to experience the convergence of person and device, which Homelands take to like fish to water. The intuitive flow of touch screen technology is really a melding of human and machine. Watch a young American Homeland at work or play on an iPad, and you see the future of that increasingly intimate relationship. Touching the screen creates a real connection between the finger and the electronic display, to the point where it's becoming increasingly difficult to define what is real. For Homelands, "virtuality" will be more real than reality in many ways.

The ultimate logical outcome of such technological intimacy is an increasingly higher level of control over the world around us. If customization was the mantra of Gen-Xers and personalization the mantra of Millennials, Homelands will live in the world of personal fusion. Where customization and personalization involve taking something someone else has created and making it more appropriate to yourself, fusion is all about creating something new out of components of something old in a very real ongoing exercise based on the understanding that the (new) whole is greater than the sum of the (old) parts.

And now…a nod to the inescapable discussion of the social media phenomenon. I won't dwell on this for more than a paragraph or two because there is already so much out there on the subject. In the context of our conversation here, it is important to recognize that the only new thing about social media is the specific technology supporting it. The idea of instant interconnectivity and communications is not, societally speaking, a new-new thing.

Social media is not a product of modern technology; it is merely the most current expression of a human fundamental. Since the days of smoke signals, drums, and whistling, humans have always yearned for—and achieved—some measure of instant communication across great distances at the individual level…allowing for point-to-point, point-to-all connections. In the Canary Islands, for example (which are named after dogs rather than birds, by the way), islanders developed a communication system consisting of whistles (understanding that high-pitched sounds travel farther and with greater clarity than shouting—the same principle is why yodeling was invented in the vast spaces of the Alps). In their own way, these folks were doing exactly what we are doing—only on a more organic, natural level; they could connect with others of their tribe and be in touch no matter where in their world they might be.

Given the probability of ever-more-enabling technology, we can expect Homelands to create truly "new-new things" out of the things around them. Given their expanding imaginations, I am literally breathless about what can come after this once they have achieved maturity and fully mastered ever-expanding technology. I am also a little frightened, to tell the truth, because as an aging Boomer I am concerned that the possibilities may well outpace the prudence.

Prudence is not at the top of the list of American characteristics—a sense of adventure is. Through the course of America's generations, beginning with the Cavalier and Glorious generations (according to Howe and Strauss), our national anthem has been closer to a song titled "Out There" from the musical *Barnum*:

Turning back should the highway bend
Turning down every chance you're given
Takes the risk out of life, but friend
How the hell can you call that livin'?
Staying put in a pumpkin shell
Is a bleak and depressing habit.
There's a ring on the carousel
And it's yours if you'll only grab it.

Reaching for the possibilities is decidedly a generational constant throughout our history to date.

Regardless of the generational moment and in spite of the apparent generational differences, the fundamental American state of mind remains identifiable as the America Code. In the end, congenitally, American generations have more in common with one another than they do with their generational counterparts around the globe. The America Code is their common ground.

PART TWO

How the America Code Plays Out Here and in the World

America is a figment of our collective imagination.
We need to be careful about what we imagine.

SECTION V

The Code and American Egonomics

THE AMERICAN ECONOMY IS A PRIME EXAMPLE of the America Code at work. One of the distinctly delightful things about working as a consultant and futurist is frequently meeting with business and thought leaders. Invariably the discussion turns to the economy. These very smart people devote much energy to studying a complex array of economic indicators, cycles, trends, variations, patterns, and projections. When times are good, they want to know how long the boom will last. When times are bad, they want to know when the pain will end.

I have found that the key to understanding the economy is an often overlooked and underappreciated simplicity: The American economy is the measurable expression of the American ego. In a very real sense we are the economy, and the economy is essentially a figment of our collective imagination. It is a measure of how we see, and how we bet on, the future. When we are successful, we spend and invest, and the economy thrives; when things start to go bad, we pull back, we stop spending and investing, and the economy spirals downward. We are simultaneously the creators and the victims of what might better be called the national *egonomy*—a manifestation of the collective American ego.

We suffer more from economic woes than we should, but our collective congenital amnesia keeps us from realizing that simply learning from our collective past misadventures will help us regain control of the present and the future. The longer we don't act, the worse the situation gets. We are often our own worst economic enemies—but it doesn't have to be that way.

CHAPTER 50

American Egonomics: We Have Met the Economy and It Is Us

TO PARAPHRASE THE COMIC STRIP CHARACTER POGO, who in his turn paraphrased Oliver Hazard Perry, a naval hero of the War of 1812, "We have met the economy, and it is us!" After all is said and done, the

American economy is a figment of our collective and uniquely American imagination—a tangible expression of the American ego. We *are* the economy. The facts and figures in the press are no more and no less than a list of the symptoms. The "condition" itself is a measure of how we bet the future.

Some might say that the economy is a reflection of our collective sense of self, but I believe the truth is more literal. We feel exuberant, we feel depressed, and every point in between. Based on those feelings, we act out. We put a value on what is essentially an unchanging reality based mainly on those feelings. When we are bummed out, we sell. When we are cheerfully optimistic, we buy.

Take the stock market, for example. The market is based on the notion that one person, convinced that a stock has nowhere to go but down, needs to find another person who is equally convinced that it has nowhere to go but up. As long as this optimism/pessimism equation remains in balance, the market works. When the equation is disrupted because more pessimistic egos enter the market, the result is a bad economy, a recession, a correction, a burst bubble. The pundits report that "the economy" or "the market" has done this or done that. In fact, they are reporting on what we Americans have or have not done—the economic impact is the result of our disposition. The problem is that reporting this as a kind of independent, third-party activity disconnects the results from the actual cause—*us!*

Some would say that this idea represents a gross oversimplification. On the other hand, I believe that seeing something as very complicated or very difficult is another way of saying "It's really beyond me" and gives each of us license not to act—or to leave the action to others who should know better than we. If something is really, *really* complicated, we have an excuse for not doing something to affect it—but not acting is also an action. When we pull out of the market, the effect is negative and starts the downward spiral.

"Come on," you might be thinking, "can something as complex as our national economy really be that simple?" At its most elemental level, the answer is a decided "yes." Take, for example, Warren Buffett, chair of and wizard behind Berkshire Hathaway, a company that seems to succeed whether times are good or bad.

What makes WB so incredibly astute at investing? According to Mr. Buffett himself, it's very simple: The secret is "buy low and sell high." He has also been known to say, *It's far better to buy a wonderful company at a fair price than a fair company at a wonderful price*—which some would also view as gross oversimplification. In his case, the thinking clearly stands the test of time.

Mr. Buffett's success comes from keeping the formula simple. Everything is a matter of timing. The key, as Mr. Buffett no doubt appreciates, is knowing what "low" is and when "high" is about to happen and what is "fair" and when. To understand that, let's take a look at American egonomics at work over the past 200 years or so.

CHAPTER 51

Why When We Feel Bad the Economy Feels Bad

It is all about ego and attitude. When we feel bad, the economy gets bad, which makes us feel worse. When we feel worse, we act accordingly. The result is that the economy gets increasingly worse, in an ever-descending spiral. That is precisely why the country's leaders need to be careful about what they say in public and how they say it. When certain circumstances occur, politicians naturally gravitate toward overstatement on the theory that the worse things seem to be, the more likely whatever they do will be seen as having some positive effect in the end. Overplaying the "bad" card also gives politicos greater license to act "for the common good."

Not coincidentally, when a sitting president says things are really, really bad, economically at least, they typically get worse the next day. If you want to have an economic downturn accelerated and turbocharged, simply have the chief executive go on television every day to talk about how grave the crisis is and how drastic the measures required to fix it. As the message sinks in, ever-increasing numbers of people will invariably get out of the market to wait until things bounce back. The very act of abstention has a direct negative effect. The more people get out of the market, the more the economy drops and the longer any recovery will take. The stock market and the state of the economy are inexorably linked. Decisions to buy or sell stock are made according to how we bet the future. Those decisions inevitably express themselves in the state of the economy at large.

CHAPTER 52

Every Five Years a Recession—Count on It!

As THIS BOOK IS BEING WRITTEN, the United States is in the throes of a recovery from what is sometimes described by the media as the Great Recession. Clearly this expression makes for good press, and clearly it is good fodder for political campaigns. In actual fact, what happened in 2008 and 2009 was not nearly as huge an economic catastrophe as some would have us believe.

American overstatement cuts both ways. We have a tendency to overstate disasters of the economic kind. The economic misadventure of 2008 has been called the "Great Recession of 2008"—putting it on a parallel with the events and circumstances of the crash of 1929. As it actually turns out, that title will probably not hold. Of the forty-seven recessionary events since 1790, the so-called Great Recession would rank twenty-seventh (see **Table 52-1** below, which lists the thirty most severe economic disruptions).

While most of the chart is self-explanatory, note that the column on the farthest right represents the degree of damage done to the economy as a result of the event. This table was compiled by National Bureau of Economic Research[17]. The estimated economic impact is based on a variable set of metrics because consistent data was neither collected nor analyzed in the same way over the 222 years since 1790.

Remarkably, or maybe not so remarkably, the worst lows have consistently followed the highest highs. If you see a rise in the economy of several hundred percent, you can be quite sure a *correction* is on the way— or at least it is waiting in the wings for a probable appearance.

Table 52-1. Recessionary Events Since 1790				
Description	Start	End	Years	Impact %
1. No Name	1839	1843	4	−34.3
2. Panic of 1873 and The Long Depression	1873	1879	6	−33.6
3. No Name	1836	1839	3	−32.8
4. No Name	1882	1885	3	−32.8
5. Depression of 1920–1921	1920	1921	1	−32.7
6. Panic of 1907	1907	1908	1	−31.0
7. Panic of 1893	1893	1894	1	−29.7
8. Great Depression	1929	1933	4	−26.7
9. No Name	1865	1867	2	−23.8
10. Panic of 1857	1857	1858	1	−23.1
11. No Name	1923	1924	1	−22.7
12. Panic of 1896	1895	1897	2	−20.8
13. No Name	1913	1914	1	−19.8
14. No Name	1847	1848	1	−19.7
15. No Name	1853	1854	1	−18.4
16. No Name	1902	1904	2	−17.1
17. No Name	1860	1861	1	−14.5
18. No Name	1918	1919	1	−14.1
19. No Name	1945	1945	0.67	−12.7
20. No Name	1890	1891	1	−11.7
21. Panic of 1910–1911	1910	1912	2	−10.6
22. No Name	1926	1927	1	−10.0
23. No Name	1869	1870	1	−9.7
24. No Name	1899	1900	1	−8.8
25. No Name	1887	1888	1	−8.2
26. No Name	1845	1846	1	−5.9
27. Great Recession	2007	2009	2	−4.1
28. No Name	1937	1938	1	−3.4
29. No Name	1957	1958	1	−3.1
30. No Name	1981	1982	1	−2.7

It is not making too much of a leap to see the connection between our optimism and the creation and contraction of what we call economic bubbles. We get enthusiastic, we get greedy, then there comes a moment of reckoning when we realize that what is happening economically is not real and not sustainable, and we lose our enthusiasm big time. That's what happened in the Rich Man's Panic of 1907, the market crash of '29, and the most recent events of 2008–2009.

The same cycle happens over and over and has happened this way since the beginning of the United States of America. It is likely to continue exactly the same way as long as human nature and the America Code conspire to keep the game in play. Our optimism gets the better of us while the collective congenital amnesia keeps us from recalling and applying the lessons of the past. Well, they would be lessons if we learned from them, that is.

CHAPTER 53

The Right to My Own Stuff

ONE OF THE MOST DISTINCTIVE AMERICAN CHARACTERISTICS and one that sets America apart is the ingrained assumption that each of us is entitled to our share of the *stuff* that matters most—the driving force behind our consumer society. In fact, it can be said that what has made America a world power is the production, distribution, marketing, and ownership of stuff by all levels of American society. The right to my own stuff has been with us from the very beginning, and our current level of consumerism is the direct by-product of World War II.

At the height of the war, we became the very essence and substance of a producing and manufacturing Goliath. We literally won that war by producing more military stuff than anyone else on the planet. When the fighting was over, that capacity for production turned to the manufacture of *stuff* for you and *stuff* for me fueled by the need to fill the homes to which we then first began to feel entitled.

In a very real sense, the right to my own stuff is an essential fundamental for a thriving democracy and contributes to peace and domestic tranquility because having a piece of the action, no matter how small, gives a citizen the sense of participation in the benefits of that democracy.

First among America's contributions to the world is a political system based on individual liberty. As Mark Twain once observed,

We are called the nation of inventors. And we are. We could still claim that title and wear its loftiest honors if we had stopped with the first thing we ever invented, which was human liberty.

But Mr. Twain didn't stick around long enough to get a gander at our twentieth-century contribution to world peace and harmony, something that is in its own way almost the latter-day equivalent of the first great American invention. You have to remember that much of the battle behind our First Revolution was about land—that is, property rights. For much of history, most of the people of every country didn't have much of a say in government because leadership was reserved only to those who owned land. The common people had no acreage so they had no right to a voice.

Even though most of our Founders were landowners, the first American Revolution was meant to give the average guy the right to own a little something along with the right to vote. Mind you, it wasn't about entitlement to ownership like the great communist principle of redistribution of wealth and land, but at least there was the possibility of buying something all your own. And that was something different indeed.

That takes us to the second American Revolution—the right and the ability to own stuff—the phenomenon of global consumerism. Certainly, over the centuries, average people have had the ability to own things— mainly clothing and personal items, as well as cooking utensils, toys, tools of a trade, pottery, and the occasional farm animal. When archaeologists dug up the ruins of Pompeii, one of the things they found was advertisements touting the sale of pocket knives for young boys—including celebrity endorsements by Roman gladiators (who should certainly have had something significant to say about knives and other weapons).

But the kind of consumerism going on since the middle of the last century is something altogether different. In fact, consumerism as we know it is a relatively recent development. It all began after the Second World War.

It doesn't take much historical training to understand that America won the war with matériel as much as fighting spirit. The fact is that our factories have never been more efficient and productive before or since.

Between 1941 and 1945 we produced some 325,000 military aircraft (roughly 180 every day of the year). Germany and Japan together came up with only about 200,000. While there were no cars being produced in Detroit during the war, the assembly lines were humming twenty-four hours a day to put out an estimated 90,000 tanks (50 per day every day of the year).

Perhaps the most remarkable accomplishment was America's production of warships and merchant vessels, an extremely important commodity for a country two oceans away from its enemies. The United States produced more than 8 million tons of military ships during the war. This was more than twice the production of everyone else involved in the war, both friend and enemy, and four times as much as Germany and Japan.

The American genius for production rose to an all-time high with the Liberty ships. As Germany, Japan, accidents, and forces of nature did a lot of damage to our merchant navy on the high seas, it was essential that every ship sunk or disabled be replaced as rapidly as possible to maintain the flow of fighting men and matériel to the different theaters of combat. The Liberty ship was invented to meet this demand. Before World War II it took as much as 14 months to custom-build a cargo vessel, assembling it piece by piece and riveting the hull one plate at a time. The Liberty ships were built in several large sections that were welded together. For all intents and purposes, they were the product of mass production techniques.

Over the course of the war, 2,710 such ships were built in eighteen different shipyards. That means 150 ships per shipyard, or roughly one ship every three months. Actual construction time was about forty-five days for a vessel of 14,000 tons and 125 feet in length that could run along at about 20 miles per hour and carry nearly 11,000 tons of cargo.

The record for building a liberty ship (the *Robert E. Peary*) was set in Richmond, California, at the Permanente Metals Corporation (Kaiser) in November 1942. At that time some 250,000 parts were turned into a ship in four days and fifteen hours. The ship was launched on November 12.

So we won the war because we figured out how to produce more military stuff than anyone else. The stage was set for the beginning of a new era in consumerism. On the one hand, there were millions of Americans who had served their country and who were given, through the GI Bill of Rights, an opportunity for affordable, government-guaranteed loans with which to buy their own homes. On the other hand was the capacity and the know-how to make all the stuff the new consumers might need.

Because the nation had geared up for combat, building anything from homes to municipal buildings was a highly developed talent in the nation. Concepts of factory production lines were quickly adapted to the production of homes and the notion of "developments" quickly followed. Levittown, New York (which singer Pete Seeger satirized in his 1961 song lyric "ticky-tacky boxes all the same") was built at the rate of eighteen 750-square-foot homes in the morning and another eighteen homes at night.

Every new home required furnishings. As comedian George Carlin once observed, "A home is a place where you put your stuff." The need for stuff for the home expanded exponentially. Luckily, or serendipitously, both the skills and the production capacity to meet the need were standing by and would otherwise have been idle after the war. Thus consumerism was born. In a very real sense, consumerism is the most tangible expression of individual liberty and the ownership of a home is its ultimate achievement of personal initiative.

The chart below tracks the evolution of "stuff" in America as expressed through our car-buying habits and rituals (see **Table 53-1**). In the 1920s and 1930s, there basically was no stuff to be had. For most Americans, getting by and staying alive were the prime directives.

In the 1940s and 1950s, the great difference between demand and supply turned the American landscape into a search for "any stuff" and eventually "the right stuff." In the first postwar years you might have the money but

Table 53.1. The Evolution of Stuff and Consumerism in America

Era	Nature of Stuff	The automobile as analogy
1920s–1930s	No stuff	IF you can afford one…
1940s–1950s	Any stuff/the right stuff	The "right" car for your station in life. The GM hierarchy of brands
1960s–1970s	Stuff with "karma"	The VW Beetle, the VW Thing
1980s	Really nice stuff	BMW, Mercedes, Porsche
1989–1994	The only stuff that I can afford	Aging personal fleets. New ways of acquiring the use of a car. Leasing.
1995–2000	The anything is possible paradox	$19,000 "luxury sedans." $45,000 "trucks" (SUVs)
2001–present	The stuff that matters most to me!	Hummer I, II, III. Lexus SUV Hybrid. Prius. Smart Car.

even that did not ensure your access to the stuff you wanted. This was a key formative period of the American consumer experience in which the upper hand belonged to the marketers who controlled availability. Consumers accepted virtually any rules to follow to get the right stuff. We spoke in another chapter about the General Motors hierarchy of starting out in a Chevy and earning your way up to the impossible dream of owning a Cadillac.

The 1960s and 1970s were the period of "stuff with karma." The things we bought needed to have an identifiable element, cachet, or specialness. Volkswagen exemplified that ideal with the lovable Beetle. Here was a car originally designed for the people (not our people, but the citizens of the Third Reich) in part by Adolf Hitler. Somehow it took on a warm and fuzzy nature and became one of the most popular automobiles on America's roads. Certainly, the low price tag helped, but this was also the period of America's value muscle cars. The Volkswagen "Thing" was an even odder phenomenon. Here was a German army staff car, painted vivid orange, that somehow became the darling of the surfer set and other really cool groups.

In the 1980s, Americans moved up a notch in the world. We sought out "really nice stuff" regardless of the price point. "Beamers, Benzes, and Porsches" became badges of accomplishment. Curiously, all three were also German-manufactured although at the exact opposite end of the price spectrum.

The economy stumbled in the first half of the 1990s, and American consumers moved painfully from "really nice stuff" to "the only stuff I can afford." Instead of trading in every three years, we let our cars get older. Something like 60 percent of US registered automobiles were more than seven years old. Forty percent were more than ten years old. This was also the period when leasing (which let you get more car for the same monthly commitment) became popular.

In the second half of the 1990s, the nature of stuff in America changed again, and we encountered the *possibility paradox* where the way we defined things made them more affordable and less intimidating. Because of the way the economy and marketers aligned, stuff was to be understood in different ways. As the luxury car companies came to the realization that they couldn't keep selling $70,000 cars and grow as a company, they redefined the idea of luxury and invented a new counterpart—"affordable luxury." All of a sudden, Mercedes Benzes came in a more compact size with a more compact price. Coming at the consumer the other way, American car companies came up with the term "luxury SUV," which is another way of saying "very expensive truck." So you could buy a truck with all the trimmings that cost about as much as a luxury car.

From about 2001 to the present and probably for the foreseeable future, each of us has learned how to buy "the stuff that matters most to me." With availability being very high and most costs having come down (thanks in large part to overseas production), we get to pick and choose among an apparently endless number of choices. Every customer satisfied, guaranteed!

CHAPTER 54

Global Consumerization – Our Other Contribution to World Peace

WITHOUT ANYONE PAYING VERY MUCH ATTENTION, it seems that Americans have given the world a second and perhaps equally, if not more significant, big idea. While we wring our hands and bemoan the fact that *globalization* is ruining us and our economy, we seem to be missing the point. The point is that globalization is not a new phenomenon at all. Rome was a global economy. Greece was a global economy. In fact, in the early 1900s, you could travel everywhere in the world without a passport and you didn't have to carry cash—a global economy.

What's happening today is not globalization, but *global consumerization*. Largely fueled by the engine of American economic expansion, more and more people around the world are enjoying a higher standard of living than at any other time in history.In ever more places around the globe, "poor" is becoming a relative rather than an absolute description.

More importantly, the benefit of global consumerization is a step toward more stable world peace. In a world where the primary concern of most citizens is consumerism, rather than seizing what others possess and they lack, and in which an ever increasing number of people have access to the possibility of a piece of the economic pie, it is very bad form (and exceptionally bad business) to go to war against your vendors or bomb your markets.

CHAPTER 55

The Ten-Dollar Jeans Conundrum

MANY AMERICANS ARE ANXIOUS about the trend toward globalization of the economy. That is why, in their 2011 book *That Used to Be Us: How America Fell Behind in the World It Invented and How We Can Come Back,* Thomas Friedman and Michael Mandelbaum argue that dealing with the challenge of globalization is one of the top four issues facing America in the future.[18]

Global consumerization is a positive force, one that has roots in our history and a place in our future. There are two aspects to the "blue jeans principle." In the first place, a German immigrant (one Levi Strauss) made a fortune and founded a garment empire with a simple idea. He innovated clothing for the miners in California's 1840s Gold Rush. He riveted pockets onto the garment for strength, used a heavier-than-usual fabric (originating in Nimes, France; hence "de Nimes" and eventually denim), and sold his goods at whatever the market would bear. Over time, the venerable blue jean pants went highbrow and high fashion. Along the way the prices rose to astronomical heights and the once-humble garment began to play a role in politics and global economics.

In fact, blue jeans contributed to the fall of the Soviet Union and have changed the relationship between us and the no-longer-strictly-communist Chinese. Some years before the fall of the Berlin Wall and the collapse of the great experiment in Russian communism, it was said that Soviet young people would trade a Lada (a Fiat-type Russian-manufactured car) for a pair of genuine American jeans (or "jeensy," as they called them). It's uncertain who actually got the better of the deal because the joke was "the jeans you could at least wear home; the car you had to push home." In the end, Soviet Russia collapsed because it had to choose between maintaining a state of Cold War with the United States or providing its own citizens with blue jeans lest they ultimately revolt.

The connection between the blue jeans principle and the changes in China is also strong. Not that long ago, communist China's driving principle was the defeat (and preferably the destruction) of the decadent West (that would be us). Today, Chinese of all ages line up at one of six Wal-Mart stores in Beijing, for example, to buy Chinese-made, American-label jeans, not to mention the range of other American-label products available in the country. From cars to toiletries to over-the-counter medicines, the Chinese have come to think of America as the Global Emporium rather than as the Great Enemy. Peace in our time? Certainly the best chance we've had in centuries.

In a way, the blue jeans principle has come full circle—creating opportunities for disadvantaged yet ambitious and diligent "foreigners"— this time beyond our shores. What drives global consumerization is the simple fact that Americans want to be able to buy a pair of jeans for ten dollars. Since we can't manufacture blue jeans that cheaply in this country, we export that manufacturing to another country where the living standard is low enough that the workers are paid so little that our jeans can be sold back in the States for ten bucks.

We did that in Japan and Mexico and Malaysia and Eastern Europe. In each case, two things happened: (a) We got our jeans, and they got jobs; and (b) they used the money from those jobs to buy increasingly better "stuff"— much of which comes from the USA.

Thus the blue jeans principle becomes an increasingly global participatory exercise in consumerization—and that's a good thing. The people of the world may not agree on politics. They may not agree on religion. But they do agree that a good pair of jeans at a good price is a good thing, and that makes everybody more alike than not—a pretty fair start for a common ground of conversation.

The one thing you can say about consumerization that you can't say about some of the other things that make people both alike and different is that it seems to have no natural boundary. In the deepest, darkest parts of the Amazon, you are likely to find a fellow wearing a Yankees T-shirt and a Red Sox baseball cap. He probably doesn't understand or appreciate the irony, but he is part of the globally consumerized planet, and he has at least some sense of who we are and what we're all about.

As a nation, we should like that because we invented consumerization and we're very good at spreading that notion. More often than not, it tends to push governments in the direction of respect (or at least tolerance) for individuality and at least a functional form of democratization such as that which has occurred in China.

CHAPTER 56

Shaking the Great Depression

IF YOU ARE A GI GENERATION AMERICAN, or a member of the Silent generation, or even a Boomer, you have a real connection to the greatest adverse event in American economic history, the Great Depression. If you did not experience the event yourself, you grew up in a household managed by those who did.

If you are a Gen-Xer, or a Millennial, or a member of the up-and-coming Homeland generation, you may not have so direct a link to what happened in the 1920s and 1930s in America, but at every economic downturn you are reminded that it is the benchmark for the worst of our expectations.

Looming behind every economic disaster or potential disaster is the specter of the "crash of 1929" and what transpired afterward. But if you take a very close look at all the things that happened during that period, ranging from an economic setback of major proportions to a literal plague of locusts and a series of weather events that were virtually apocalyptic, you begin to see that the circumstances for a new global depression would require the alignment of an incredible number of factors for the second time in human history—possible, but highly unlikely.

While I can't guarantee anything as an author or as a futurist, I can point out that the Great Depression reflected and resulted from a set of circumstances that are unlikely—no, make that highly unlikely—to repeat themselves in exactly the same order, on exactly the same scale, or in exactly the same sequence. We need to get over the Great Depression once and for all. To do that, we need to understand it, appreciate it, and work hard to ensure it has zero chance of repeating.

CHAPTER 57

Why the Great Depression Won't Ever Happen Again

ONE OF THE REASONS THE GREAT DEPRESSION STICKS OUT in our collective memory as "the" bad economic event of our history is not merely because it had such a huge impact on the American economy and society but also because it lasted so long. The period of serious economic instability and "depression" began in October 1929. Most historians and observers will agree that the effects of that day carried through into the 1950s and affected the country into the 1960s in a number of different ways. All of which explains why people get nervous about the possibility of a repeat.

What actually happened was this. In October 1929, the stock market tanked and the wealth of millions of Americans, both great and small, evaporated almost overnight. What happened next was a series of contributing circumstances and events, some literally apocalyptic, that kept grinding the ship of the American economy against a cliff of remorseless catastrophe. In each of the following three years, the economy further staggered and fell. By 1932, the Dow Jones Industrial Average stood at 50, down catastrophically from its prior high of 375.

The truth is that catastrophic collapses of the economy, as measured in part by the Dow index back in 1929, were part of a pattern that has been with us ever since we have had an economy and ever since we had a Dow with which to monitor it.

A precipitous meltdown of the Dow and the national economy was by this time nothing new. In fact, the period between 1896 (when the Dow came into being) and 1907, the index's first decade, was a roller coaster of euphoria and unprecedented catastrophe rolled into one. In 1897, the Dow started out at 40. In 1899 it nearly doubled to 75. As a result of the Rich Man's Panic in 1903, it dropped back to its original 40. By the end of 1905, the Dow was up at over 100. Two years later, as a result of the Panic of 1907, it had lost nearly half its value and hovered just a bit over 50. By the end of 1909 it had doubled back in value to sit at 100.

The truth is that there had also been panics before the Dow Jones index began tracking our economic progress—not the least of which occurred in 1893 and 1896. The pattern of ups and downs established during the first decade of the index both mirrored what had come before and pointed to what lay ahead. In spite of what the first years foreshadowed and in spite of even the greatest economic disasters to date, the economy, as measured by the Dow Jones index in this hundred-year chart, followed an inexorable straight line of upward growth (see **Figure 57-1**).

The factors that made the Great Depression different from all the other fluid economic events before or since are many and varied. This pivotal moment in American history needs to be understood in the context of a series of relevant but not necessarily connected events that dragged the misery out for nearly three decades.

100 Years of Ups and DOWns

Dow Jones Industrial Average

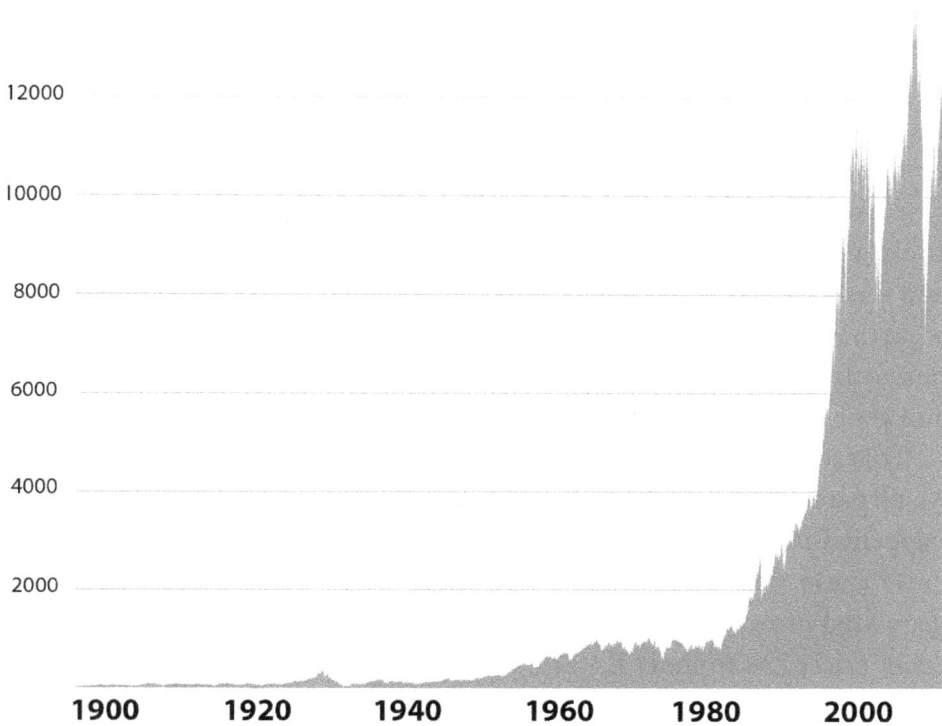

Figure 57-1. Dow Jones Industrial Averages from 1896 to 2012.

CHAPTER 58

The Apocalypse and the Dow

IN 1929, the stock market, the Dow, and the economy took a serious plunge—of that, most Americans are aware. Less understood is the fact that it took another three years to bring us to what is now known as the Great Depression—and not everything that brought about the Depression was things financial.

Before we address the down side of the Great Depression, let's take a moment to appreciate what came before and, in a sense, set up the inevitability of the crash. In the decade between 1920 and 1929, the economy was booming and the stock market was exploding. In that time, the value of Wall Street increased by more than 400 percent! As exciting as the boom appeared, it was built on the same kind of foundation that was laid before every major panic of prior decades.

Basically, people were encouraged to buy into the future—whether they could afford it or not. In the '20s, you could buy stock for 10 percent down and finance the rest. In other words, the system encouraged people to buy what they could not afford at the moment on the assumption that it would be worth enough at the time the loan came due to both pay back the interest and generate a healthy profit for the purchaser.

This was pretty much the same state of affairs that preceded the Rich Man's panic of 1903 and the Panic of 1907. It was also eerily similar to what happened in the "go-go" '80s that led to the painful reality checks of the '90s. These were not the only occasions when insupportable optimism generated growth rates as high as 400 percent increases and then led to economic catastrophes. In fact, in the decade before 2008, the United States once again experienced 400 percent growth, fueled largely by the fact that Americans were encouraged to purchase homes that they could not then afford, on the assumption that the value of the homes would escalate to more than cover the original sales price and generate a profit for the purchaser.

So why is it unlikely that another Great Depression with an exceptionally prolonged recovery period is waiting out there for us? To answer that, we need to go back to 1933, a year in which two pivotal events contributed to a prospective turn-around in America. In that year Franklin Delano Roosevelt first became president and, as it happens, in the same year, Prohibition was repealed. A palpable sense of relief and a return of optimism accompanied both events in some measure.

Sure enough, the economy began a recovery. Unfortunately, this rebound was severely dampened by a natural disaster of biblical proportions. A massive drought had hit the nation's midsection and continued for the next six years. As a result of over-farming and the loss of water, much of the

Midwest's fertile topsoil dried to a powder and was blown away, devastating farms and the nation's food supply.

If Americans had felt chastised for the over-optimism and sinful excesses of the Roaring Twenties by the crash of 1929, the blow to America's food supply felt much more significant and cut closer to the soul. The dust that was once topsoil was blown in great choking clouds all the way across the country. The great History Channel special *America: The Story of US* offered a clip of the Statue of Liberty in New York Harbor virtually obscured by a dust storm that likely originated as far west as Kansas or even Texas.

While the dust was either settling or blowing, a true plague of the biblical sort hit the American heartland with a cruel one-two punch. Locusts, millions of them, encouraged by the newly dry and hot climate in the southern and western states, ranged across the landscape, completely devastating crops and anything green and edible, causing misery and loss everywhere they went, and they went everywhere in massive flying hordes.

For the people of America, it was beginning to feel like the end of days. From financial collapse to climatic disaster to apocalyptic plague—it seemed as if the universe was throwing everything at them to test their faith. Just as these calamities appeared to be winding down, in 1936 and 1937 the heavens opened up to pour down their fury on the country—literally. In the course of two years, unprecedented numbers of floods (sparked in part by the dried-up earth's inability to soak up any rains) and an exceptional season of destructive and fatal tornadoes punished the American heartland once more. Meanwhile, on the East Coast, the great Hurricane of 1937 drowned much of the area between Connecticut and Maine and leveled literally millions of trees throughout the area. This, too, was catastrophe on an unimaginable scale.

By 1938, Americans had learned to accept and deal with the apparently endless series of really bad things that had been coming their way. They had endured the worst that man and nature could throw at them and they were beginning to feel that the worst was over. If it had been, perhaps the American economy might have taken a sharp upturn. As it was, there were more depressing turns in the road ahead.

By 1939 it had become obvious to all but the densest among us that the world was in serious trouble. With the worst sort of dictators in power—

Hitler in Germany, Franco in Spain, Stalin in Russia, Tojo in Japan, and Mussolini in Italy—there was never really an option to avoid conflict. Understandably, after a very rough decade, most Americans just wanted to sit this one out, lick their wounds, and work on their own country and their own futures. But that was not to be, beginning with the invasion of Poland on the first of September in 1939—the starting date for World War II as our eventual allies saw it.

Reluctantly, a resigned populace entered that war a little over two years later when the Japanese made it impossible to ignore their attack on Pearl Harbor on December 7, 1941. At the end of the war, in 1945, America's young men were ready to wind down their duty as soldiers and come back home to pick up the pieces of their lives. Instead, they found themselves in a new and, as it turned out, much more extended kind of conflict. This was the ideological battle between democracy and totalitarianism, between the United States and our allies on one side, and the Soviet Union and China on the other.

This time, the stakes were higher, including the possible annihilation of all life on the planet. From an ego point of view, the fight for survival occupied most of our time, our national treasures, and our lives from 1939 well into the 1970s. Virtually every day during that time, the sword of Damocles hung over all our heads. At any moment the world could end and us with it. Clearly not a good time to focus on such basics as economics or worry about the future since there was a real chance there would not be one.

These are the facts that surrounded the Great Depression and defined all it eventually came to mean to Americans. As the full story suggests, a great many significant events before and after 1929 contributed to the impact of what started out as a relatively simple financial disaster, one in a chain that preceded it and followed it, and eventually became a prolonged national agony with many dimensions—most of them bad.

CHAPTER 59

We Keep Doing It to Ourselves

IF THE CRASH OF 1929 was more of an extreme example of a recurring egonomic phenomenon than a singularly devastating event, then what's the rule and how does ego play a part in our economic cycles? The answer to that question is illustrated by the graph below (see **Figure 59-1**).

Because we are a nation of incurable optimists, something (most commonly a conscious, precipitating action or intent by someone with something to gain) spurs a period of unbridled and unsustainable exuberance. We create and claim opportunities and possibilities that simply aren't grounded in reality.

The crash is actually more of a correction—a normal process that resets the values of the market and the economy to where they should be or should have been all along. Eventually that new value is consistently higher than what it might have been without the sharp although unrealistic boost that precedes it. Eventually, the correction bottoms out (usually within two to three years), we achieve somewhere between 90 and 120 percent of

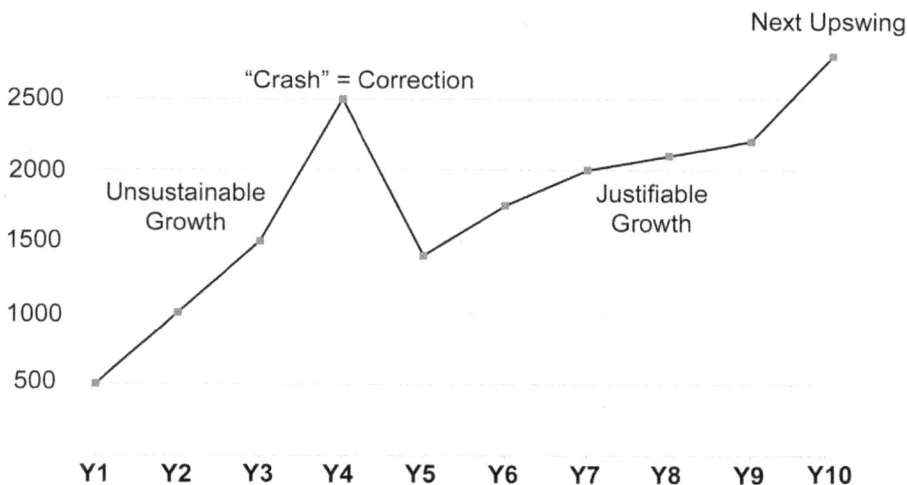

Figure 59-1. The Recessionary Cycle.

the previous high, and off we go again on a period of realistic, sustainable economic growth fueled by fact rather than fancy.

Driven by a large population of Mechanists and because we become impatient with the norm, someone eventually games the new standard to create new opportunities—and the cycle begins anew. The inevitability of repeating the cycle is part of the American experience, both because our egos require getting more than we have a right to expect from realistic calculation and because we are a country that favors extremes, bold colors, and bold initiative.

But then, if we had allowed ourselves to be limited by mere realities at critical points in history, this would not be America and we would not be Americans. That is one of our national dilemmas—how to reconcile what we want something to be versus what circumstances say it should be. The answer is that we don't. Over the course of more than 200 years, that attitude has been generally more productive and more valuable than sitting on the sidelines waiting for the real world to line up and provide us with realistic opportunities.

While the Rich Man's Panic of 1903 was disastrous to many, it also made possible the funding of the railroads that created a connective steel tissue from east to west and north to south, making of us a truly united nation in social, economic, and political terms. While the crash of 1929 similarly shattered the dreams of many, it did in fact provide capital for some of the companies that ultimately defined America's post–World War II position of leadership in the world.

There were several curiously serendipitous side effects of the Great Depression and its accompanying natural disasters and massive unemployment. One was the creation of the Works Projects Administration, which built most of the aging infrastructure on which we still rely. WPA engineers and workers built everything from secondary and primary bridges, to Connecticut's Merritt Parkway, to the vast Tennessee Valley Authority flood control project. Another "benefit" of the disastrous '30s was the creation of a large force of young men who learned to live in barracks, work together under dire circumstances, and put the group ahead of themselves. Many of the young men who joined the Civilian Conservation Corps of the '30s found themselves in familiar territory when the country went to war in 1941. This history is one of the reasons America was able to mount an effective fighting force so quickly, in spite of the fact that we had only a volunteer army and limited production capacity in the very first days of that war.

Whether and how we eventually get to a "good" result from a "bad" event, at some point we recognize that this unbridled enthusiasm simply cannot continue because it is fundamentally built on hope and ego rather than on reality. That moment is the first sign of the crash, collapse, or financial catastrophe that lies ahead.

SECTION VI

Coming to Grips with Change

CHANGE AND THE FUTURE GO HAND IN HAND. You can't plan for the future without first coming to grips with the concept of change. Change is another conundrum with which Americans grapple. As optimists, we see change as an opportunity for something better. At the same time, anything we cannot directly control or adequately understand makes us uncomfortable. This discomfort can turn to fear when words and phrases such as "unprecedented," "game-changing," or "America will never be the same again" are thrown into the conversation.

What does it take to embrace change and learn how to profit from it? First you need a model that reassures rather than intimidates—one that connects the past, present, and future in a seamless, understandable flow. No matter how different something at first appears, ultimately, up will pop something familiar about the situation. Taking the right historical perspective makes virtually every change manageable, if not downright welcome.

The other key to dealing with change is learning to understand the difference between what is inevitable (such as cycles and processes of expansion and contraction) and what is true change. Once you separate these two concepts, the change will be much less daunting because at least one of the two will be consistently predictable—the dirty little professional secret of us working futurists.

Understanding the true nature of change is like understanding the fundamentals of driving or golf—once you do, you naturally become a better driver or golfer. Seeing yourself as the driver of change rather than its unwitting passenger can go a long way toward creating a feeling of comfort and control about the future.

CHAPTER 60

A Comforting Model for Change

CHANGE. IS IT CONTINUAL AND ETERNALLY EXPANSIVE? Is it something else? If you buy into Einstein's theory ($e = mc^2$), then nothing is created new and nothing is destroyed with any meaningful finality. Matter turns into energy. Energy turns back into matter…and the great wheel of the cosmos grinds on and on. So here's a question: If the universe itself works in a cycle where nothing is completely new yet nothing stays exactly the same, and biological life works the same way (it does), then what kind of arrogance leads us to believe that the works of humanity somehow follow a separate set of laws? Arrogance of the worst and most ignorant kind, indeed! As I have come to appreciate, the fundamental nature of change is that things go back to new places.

The reason we don't see that clearly is that, for most of us, the future is scary. That is because in order for the future to become the future, things have to change. Most of us are not comfortable with change for the very simple reason that we assume change to be, almost by definition, what cannot be known. We fear what we do not know as a matter of natural human emotionality.

The best way to get a handle on change and to be comfortable with it is to understand what change really is. Perhaps the most positive way to approach change so that it is neither scary nor uncontrollable is to think of it in terms of *things going back to new places.*

I have developed this perspective as a working futurist—someone who tries to help people get to a better place by learning to be in command of and comfortable with change. Over more than two decades, I have found the point of view to be both calming and energizing.

CHAPTER 61

Change: Things Going Back to New Places

WE FEAR THE FUTURE because we see change in the context of a road that runs off into the distance. Immediately in front of us the road is clear and understandable. Off in the mid-distance, it pops in and out of trees and turns and hills, but we get a general sense of its direction, progress, and condition. Once it gets too far out ahead of us and disappears over the farthest hill or into the biggest forest, we have no "feel" for where it's headed. For all we know, without a map or reports from travelers who have gone before us and come back to tell the tale, the road could simply vanish. In the extreme, the road could literally lead to the end of the earth as we know it and take us into some desolate distant desert...or worse.

Clearly, this view is, on the one hand, not particularly comforting, and on the other, not particularly useful. It doesn't tell us how to act. It simply lies there as a vision that can fill us with fear and incite us to inaction.

A more dynamic and somewhat comforting way of seeing change involves thinking of it as a continual rebalancing—as if everything that happens is part of some natural equilibrium. First things go one way and then they swing back to where they began...endlessly repeating the same patterns over and over again. An appropriate visual for this perspective might be the pendulum of an old-fashioned clock. First it swings to the right, then back to the left, then back to the right, and so on. When the energy of a swing in one direction is expended, good old dependable gravity reverses the flow in a nice, neat, diametric return until that swing's energy is depleted...on and on ad infinitum. It is comforting to think and say that the pendulum is swinging back to what is presumably a better direction. Funny thing—when we talk about things going "back," there's usually an underlying feeling that this means a return to something knowable—the "good old day" presumption.

The problem with the pendulum view is that it is too neat, too orderly, and too limiting to describe the world as we actually feel it. The pendulum theory of change also implies and requires that things be completely reversed as they move in either direction. It allows for no progress, simply for a predetermined action in a strictly defined space in one direction followed by its exact opposite in the other.

Staying with the clock analogy, we move on to try another model for change. This is the "what goes around comes around" view. As the hands of a clock go around its face, we measure both progress over time and a kind of "return." Every twelve hours the big hand and the little hand return to the twelve o'clock position. The fact that there are two hands that travel related yet different patterns helps to get us closer to the complexity of change in our world and is a fine elevation to our thinking. It allows for a sense of progress and introduces the idea of cycles. Every twelve or twenty-four hours, we repeat a cycle. Unfortunately, while this perspective is better than the overly simplistic pendular perspective, it still presumes a fixed limit on where things can go. Life *is* the clock.

There is a fourth way to understand change—one that takes into account some form of "return" yet allows room for the introduction of true change, in the process helping to explain why even the most current circumstances often have a sense of familiarity if not literally déjà vu. Take for example the story of a chief executive who comes to power as a virtual savior. As he rises to his country's leadership, some literally consider him godlike. He is the hope and change for which his nation longs. Two short years later things sour severely. He is at odds with the legislative branch of government. The treasury is depleted. The nation finds itself increasingly dependent on foreign sources for key commodities. At the same time, credit is extremely tight and entitlements spiraling out of control. While the story seems modern, the chief executive in question is Julius Caesar, Emperor of Rome. That leader eventually suffered the ultimate penalty at the hands of his legislature and lost his life along with his office.

The fourth way is most appropriate to account for the fact that Caesar's challenges have a very strong, almost eerie familiarity about them yet allows that they are, and need to be, somehow different from that which we are experiencing today. I have found that the rolling wagon wheel gets me to that level of insight.

As the wagon wheel turns it sort of resembles the face of a clock and is clearly cyclic in nature. If you put a chalk mark at the 12 o'clock position on the wagon wheel, that chalk mark goes around through all the divisions of a clock face and eventually winds up back at the 12 o'clock position. The difference is that each time the wheel makes a complete circuit, the wagon moves to a new place. What the analogy tells us is that maybe the best way to understand change is to see it for what it is—change is "things going back to new places."

Let's talk about the idea of things going "back." Everything in nature follows the same cyclic pattern. It appears, it grows, it matures, it declines, it disappears, most often to be replaced by something that follows the same pattern in its turn. Even this pattern of succession is a form of cycle. The pattern is true of living things, inanimate objects (for example, the accretion and erosion of rocks), movements, ideas, and, as is increasingly clear, the universe itself. We recognize this inevitability in religious thinking—"ashes to ashes and dust to dust." We talk about it in health care—"cradle to grave." As we have seen in the our discussion on the subject of American egonomics, we track the universal pattern over time in the expansions and deflations of our economy.

The philosopher George Santayana said in 1905[19] (although a lot of other people get credit for the quote, including President Woodrow Wilson in 1912), *Those who cannot remember the past are condemned to repeat it.* As it turns out, old George lifted the phrase from Edmund Burke, who in about 1760 said, *Those who don't know history are destined to repeat it.* Well, you get the point: some ideas are so good they are worth repeating…and they are repeated because they continue to apply over time.

Our collective congenital amnesia keeps us from being as keenly aware of the cyclical nature of change as we might otherwise be. That means we tend to repeat mistakes that we don't need to be repeat. We also devote a good portion of our natural inventiveness to inventing new solutions rather than only inventing what is truly new and simply revising what has proven to work in the past. By appreciating that change and the future are more familiar than they are novel, we can continually build on our knowledgebase as a people. In the end, we benefit from the learning of those who preceded us, and we have that much more energy to deal with true change—not to mention we are better equipped to identify that true change for what it is.

PART THREE

Laying Out the Road We Choose to Travel Forward

Change doesn't merely happen; it is architected.
The future is a trap of our own design.

SECTION VII

Tools for Shaping the Future

IN MAKING CHOICES TOWARD THE FUTURE, we can take one of two paths. We can choose the great highway of pessimism, which assumes that things will only get worse. Or we can choose the road of optimism, which assumes that things have at least a chance of getting better. Optimism is the only route to a positive future for America and Americans because it embraces the possibility for improving every situation if we will only decide to try. By continually reminding ourselves that the future is the product of our decisions, we take more responsibility for making those decisions and leverage more control over the future.

I believe that things are easier to manage if we understand how the pieces fit together. I have come up with a formula for the future that works for individuals as much as it does for the country. In this section, I will share that formula and show you how to use it to shape the future you deserve for yourself and for the country. I will also share some prognostications about where I believe America is headed that I hope will provide some new perspectives on your part in designing and building our collective national future.

CHAPTER 62

Defining the Future

BASED ON THOUSANDS OF INTERVIEWS and conversations in which I got to ask the question "What is the future?" I have come to understand that for most Americans, the future is one of three things:

1. It is *something we can't know.*

2. It is *what happens next.*

3. It is *what we make of it* (the least common response).

The first two answers disturb me because they imply that we have no control over the future and are consigned to experience it without exerting any influence over it. The third is encouraging, because it at least embraces the premise that we have some measure of control over or capacity to shape the future, even it doesn't conveniently come with an action plan to make it so.

In the course of my work, I have come to understand that defining and getting to the future you deserve is a two-step process. The first step involves a full and honest appraisal of where you are today. The second step is visioning your desired destination in time.

The key to making that future happen is to understand how the future gets to be the future for you as a person and for the country as a whole. Finally, you need a mechanism, a process, a formula that starts the process, keeps you on track, and ultimately delivers your desired future.

CHAPTER 63

An Original Formula for the DIY Future

NO WORTHWHILE BOOK ON AN ENTIRE NATION would be complete without an attempt to look at the future. Especially as we have spent considerable time looking at the past and examining the present—and I am a futurist. Rather than just jumping out there into what is yet to be, it might be worthwhile taking a look at how the future gets to be the future in the first place.

Like most people, you probably devote way too much time trying to understand the future and too little time working on creating it. In either case you end up with the future you deserve. If you at least try to define your future on your terms, you get a chance to control it.

To make this clear, I will provide a dramatically austere and concise formula for the future. Your future. America's future. The singular and collective future of mankind and the planet. After arming you with a mechanism for creating the future you deserve, we'll take a shot at some prognostications for America's future.

I believe that things are a little easier to manage if you can reduce them to a formula that shows you how the pieces fit together. What follows below is my version of a formula for the future (see **Figure 63-1**).

In this formula, the future (F) is a result of the sum of your intentions (i) multiplied by the amount of energy (e) available to each intention. My experience is that every intention draws down the available pool of energy you possess. The more intentions or ideas you have, the less energy each one gets. The less energy it gets, the less chance it will be actualized.

That's your end of controlling the future. As it happens, there are many other people also vying with the universe to actualize their intentions. To be functionally valuable, any formula for the future needs to take into account the reality that others are projecting the future they deserve. The extent to which you can actualize your future depends on understanding and allowing for the impact of their versions of the future on your version of the future. This is taken into account by the part of the formula below the line.

To make all this work as you intend, your focus requires clarity (understanding exactly what it is that you want to take place) and prioritization (deciding which intentions matter most, which matter least, and all points in between, and deciding which intentions, in which order, are worthy of the energy you have available).

Finally, the one variable that you do not control is the intentions of others (which may either abet or diminish your own purpose) and the amount of energy with which they pursue those intentions. While you are busy pushing your own agenda with the greatest clarity and at maximum efficient energy, you also have to continually monitor the world beyond your sphere of control and planning. Keep a sharp eye out for others who might be allies or competitors. Identify them. Monitor them continually, and adapt your own plans accordingly and realistically.

$$F = \frac{(i)^e}{((i)^e)\ \text{Others}}$$

Figure 63-1. A formula for the future.

CHAPTER 64
_____

Relevant Prognostications from a Futurist

WHAT'S THE POINT OF READING A BOOK written by a futurist (especially one who includes a formula for the DIY future) unless there's also a peek at what lies ahead? What come next are a number of prognostications based on my professional experience and a healthy appreciation of the America Code at work.

- America won't be as different in the future as some people would have us believe; at least the fundamentals and defining principles are more likely to be familiar than alien if you know what you're looking at and for. Increasingly though, we'll be seeing pre-Americanized immigrants who are likely to reverse-hyphenate their national identity—holding on to the best of where they came from and connecting it to the best of the United States. As I see it, an American Pole is a significantly different creature from a Polish-American. I see the strong duality of identity as a good thing going forward.

- On the economic front, we are going to ramp up the idea of consumerism and make a major shift from owning stuff to paying to use it instead. We can also see the probability that the American economy of the future is going to be a lot more informal and less centralized. That is partly because US small business is going to be playing an increasingly critical role in that economy. There is a possibility that we may not need big business in America any more.

- Going forward, we Americans are more likely to be paid for what we create or produce rather than for what job title we bear—in a kind of piecework 2.0 economy redux. In the early days of the industrial revolution, factory workers were not paid on the basis of the time they clocked on the job but on the basis of the number of "pieces" of work they turned out during the work day. In a kind of an organic metric of productivity, each worker was paid according to his or her individual initiative, talent, and capability. Going forward, a parallel model will reward those who achieve rather than those who show up. This will simultaneously require a more self-motivated workforce and provide workers with an opportunity to determine the circumstances under which they choose to do that work.

- On a global front, the China Reckoning (the day when America's outstanding debt to China comes due) will ultimately be resolved through the Trump Gambit. The Trump Gambit goes something like this: "If I borrow a million dollars and can't pay it back—that is my problem. If I borrow a trillion dollars and can't pay it back—that is your problem." It implies that if a problem becomes large enough it is everyone's problem. This was the same principle (too big to fail) behind the rationale for saving General Motors and some of our biggest banks during the 2008 Recession (aka the Great Bailout of '08). If the model works for billion-dollar global concerns, it surely will work for trillion-dollar international bailouts.

CHAPTER 65

America Won't Be That Different in 2056

IF YOU BUY INTO THE NOTION that human progress is cyclical and that the future (or change) is all about things going back to new places, then America is not likely to end up in some dramatically unknowable place (unless, of course, those who intend for that to happen overrule those who like America pretty much as it has always been and are willing to put in the energy required to keep it that way).

The economic fundamentals (if we are the economy and if we stay pretty much the same, the economy will continue pretty much as it has for the past 250 years) will continue to operate in the same way they have since 1790. We will have recessions every five years or so. We will have recoveries. Every time the economy takes a major upward leap (on the order of 400 percent or so), count on having a major correction to bring things back on track.

We will continue to have immigrant disenfranchised diligent optimists showing up on our shores and reminding us of the blessings and wonders we enjoy here. Human nature being what it is, we will need such continual reminders over the coming centuries.

The country is certainly large enough to accommodate population growth, rich enough in natural resources, and blessed with an abundance of Advocates and Mechanists to keep things interesting in the future.

Thanks to the political system in which we are grounded and the fact that consensus is not our natural propensity, it will be difficult to keep America at any extreme for long before our natural social-political centering counterweight puts things "right."

I don't expect everything to be rosy and Pollyannaish, but I do expect the fundamental America Code to continue expressing and reasserting itself at key moments in the future.

For those readers who think me too optimistic, please consider two things. First, I operate on the America Code; I am programmed for optimism. Second, the alternatives to optimism are—well, not really alternatives for anyone so encoded.

CHAPTER 66

A Cultural Shift from Acquisition

THE NATURE OF CONSUMERISM is being transformed from the current acquisition model to a pure consumption consumerism model. Traditional consumerism assumes that people commit to products and services irrevocably. They acquire them, take possession of them, and commit to them for the long haul. In the next two decades, consumers will be more focused on making use of things—that is, getting the most out of products without being fully committed to keeping them as they age, obsolesce, or degrade.

The consumption may be long-term or it may be for short-term relationships only. The consumption model of economics achieves two intersecting goals. On the one hand, consumers (shifting from unconditional loyalty to transactional loyalty) want goods and services only for so long as those meet their ever-changing needs and desires. Under the traditional possession model, everything to which consumers commit obsolesces with increasing rapidity as they want to move on. As they move on, the problem of what to do with the things they no longer want increases.

In the new consumption model of economics, the processes of recycling, refabrication, and refurbishing remain in the control of the manufacturers and marketers—simplifying those processes and centralizing them in a way that our current model of buy-use-dump-at-a-public-facility can never achieve. Consumers will not have to take things to the town dump or to the recycling center since they will be paying for use rather than taking actual outright ownership. The corporations providing these products will also provide an infinitely more efficient system for repossessing them and economically reprocessing them. Consumption consumerism both solves the consumers' desires and makes it easier to efficiently absorb and repurpose the obsolete and the unwanted.

Think of this as an era in which products, even durable goods and automobiles, will be provided to Americans as a service. Zipcars are already changing the nature of the relationship between cars and drivers from long-term marriage to serial dating. The same model can (and likely will) apply to refrigerators, lawn tractors, even computers.

CHAPTER 67

Toward a Less Formal Economy

AS MORE AND MORE CITIZENS OF THE PLANET begin to share in the second American revolution of global consumerization, it will be increasingly impossible to maintain a central planning model for any aspect of the economy at home and abroad.

The great lesson that we should take from the Chinese democratization of the last decade or so is that the ideology of the collective good at the expense of the individual has failed again. The Chinese leadership did not move toward the mantra that "greed is good" and embrace a commercialized Hong Kong because they were somehow magically enlightened and suddenly developed an appreciation of the value of individual liberty. Instead, these ultimate pragmatists recognized that, in a world where the continuing desire for "a little piece of the action all my own" is the fundamental driver of the most proactive and influential segments of any society (the disenfranchised diligent optimists of every nation), getting millions of citizens to toe the party line is simply not going to be sustainable over the long haul.

Russian communism collapsed for very much the same reason—a centralized economic ideology couldn't compete (and can't ever compete) with individual enterprise and initiative except by force and not for long. Both the Soviet and the Chinese centrally planned economies were an imposed and unnatural layer attempting to replace the course of normal human commerce. In the end, both systems eventually and predictably succumbed to the natural forces of individual initiative.

The only part of both economic systems that remained vital throughout was what they referred to as the black market but what was simply the natural informal economy of supply and demand—uncontrolled, functional, and dynamic.

Over the next twenty years or so, America's future is likely to be influenced by an increasingly informal economy for a number of reasons.

In the first place, it is a fundamental inconsistency for Americans to accept a disenfranchising economic system that replaces individual initiative with just another form of central planning—socially, politically, or economically. I don't think most of us are planning to uproot and emigrate again, so that battle will be waged at home. For the first time in history, individuals have the upper hand over big bureaucracy in many critical spheres.

There is a new infrastructure of distributive manufacturing (in the form of contracted production anywhere on earth) that makes it possible for anyone to produce virtually anything without having to make prohibitively huge investments in facilities and personnel. Those who invest in production facilities provide the service of manufacturing to those with something to manufacture.

The existence of universal distribution infrastructure (in the form of FedEx, UPS, DHL, and others) makes it possible for a team of any five or ten clever people to become a global provider virtually overnight to virtually anywhere on the planet.

The ubiquity of web-based sales and marketing can turn a good idea into a great business with the same ease—locally, nationally, and globally.

Big business, in search of improving margins, economies of scale, and cost efficiencies, is actively reducing its ability to create the jobs of the future. As more jobs will be needed, big business is less likely to have the resources to provide them.

The once and future hope of the American economy will be America's small business owners, who today already provide a disproportionate share of new jobs, patents, innovation, and positive balance of payments.

In the next decades, we will need to rethink the whole idea of "small business." The name implies a comparison with its big brother and all that involves. There is a kind of silent assumption that the goal of every small business is to grow bigger and that growth is the natural imperative of every enterprise.

In the next few decades, that assumption will not only be challenged; it will be seriously modified, with the result that our formal, essentially centralized model of economics will need to be redefined into a more dynamic, less conventional, and decidedly more informal model.

For one thing, the 26 million Americans who are currently designated "sole proprietors" in the latest census will get their due recognition as the powerful American economic engine they represent. Since big business can't, and government shouldn't, meet the burgeoning need for new jobs in the next score years, millions more Americans will have to create their own economic opportunities. Creating a job for yourself is still creating a job; only the nature of the economy changes in the process as ever more Americans begin to do it for themselves rather than relying on the archaic traditional models of the past for providing conventional employment.

Fully portable benefits and health care will become increasingly necessary as a standard way of doing things. The new model will not be traditional employment based on getting paid for showing up at a location for a specified number of hours. Instead, tomorrow's new breed of self-employed will be paid for the work they produce regardless of the time involved, in a kind of "piecework" revisited. They will control their own time, establish their own pay rates (in a highly competitive environment), and market their services through a wide-reaching web-based "employment" exchange. Some of the time they will do the work from home; at other times they will take up temporary residence wherever the work needs to be done.

The other trend in making a living in America will be "passion-centric" gainful employment. America's Millennials are already beginning to shape this phenomenon. Many, in the course of their college years, discover a passion for something—whether it be the environment, a social cause, or providing some kind of service to others. As the cost of entry into this type of "doing what you love to do" is low, virtually anyone can find a way to get in the game.

You can start a blog to which others sharing your passion might subscribe. You might find a source for merchandise that relates to your passion. You might sell advertising space on your blog. In the increasingly fractured and splintered world of marketing, where reaching a highly targeted audience through mass media is prohibitively expensive, the opportunity for a micromedia platform centering around a passionate proponent and her "followers" will provide opportunities for the blogger and for anyone involved in the blogging platform with her. Basically, more and more individual Americans will make a decent living trafficking in information about their own passion—made possible by the web and paid for by others with similar interests.

Such a do-it-yourself economy is, by design, more difficult to understand, to measure, and to control—all of which resonates completely with the fundamental America Code. Such redefined small businesses will be the backbone of the economy in the next twenty years, reshaping the relationship between work, society, and government as they account for 70 percent or more of America's GDP in the years ahead.

CHAPTER 68

We May Not Need Big Business Anymore

BIG BUSINESS WAS CREATED because some things—colonizing a continent, building railroads, damming rivers, waging wars, and such—all needed large centrally controlled enterprises. Big has served us relatively well over the years.

The problem with big business is that at some point big businesses make big mistakes. Those big mistakes have big consequences—and because the enterprise is so big, we all end up sharing in the suffering and directly or indirectly paying for the big mistakes.

The other dangerous thing that big business has going for it is this: Once you spool up a big enough organization, it tends to roll forward whether it should or not. It eats up resources to keep itself in motion. It makes promises it can't keep and expectations it can't deliver.

The automobile companies are a perfect example. In the beginning, they contributed to the growth of our economy and the fulfillment of the American Dream. In fact, they helped to shape that American Dream. In the end, although they had become critical to our economy, they were not operating at peak performance. Companies such as General Motors had effectively gone out of business some time ago; they had simply not run out of money until recently. When such a big business falls, it falls hard and does a great deal of damage all around.

The future, I believe, belongs to a more distributive economic system. Instead of creating top-heavy mega-enterprises, smaller, more adaptable, and more flexible "component" enterprises will work together to achieve specific tasks and then reconfigure appropriately when those tasks change. In that way, we can still get big jobs done, but we will no longer perpetuate the entities created to complete them beyond obsolescence.

CHAPTER 69

Trend toward Reverse-Hyphenated Immigrants

For most of our nation's history, what you ended up with when Irish immigrants came to America was Irish-Americans—in other words, Americans with a heritage that connected them to Ireland.

In the coming decades, largely as a result of the conscious effort to respect and celebrate diversity in America and coupled with the trend toward pre-Americanized waves of immigrants, future immigration will bring to America a new kind of citizenry. As "American-Poles," for example, these reverse-hyphenated immigrants will continue to be more connected to their home country than in the past. At the same time, they will be fully invested in the American experience—largely because they share the America Code in common with the waves that preceded them.

More importantly, thanks to modern travel and communications, along with the American phenomenon of global consumerization, many if not most immigrants heading our way are effectively pre-Americanized. They have both direct and virtual experience with America and the American way of doing things. This is often, in fact, the impetus that takes them across the sea in the first place.

The children of such immigrants are even more likely to completely "Americanize" almost from birth. At the same time they will continue to connect to and relate to the country of their origin.

CHAPTER 70

The China Reckoning

One of our greatest concerns as I write this book is the China solution. How can we square the fact that we are the world's single remaining superpower, yet we are so heavily indebted to other nations and to the Chinese in particular?

Frankly, we are indebted to others because we can't seem to accept the notion that if you spend more money than you make, you will always be in debt. This simple reality applies to individuals and families. It applies to corporations, and it totally applies to nations.

The real issue is the matter of scale. At the individual level, at the family level, and certainly at the level of small business, continuing to borrow beyond your means eventually leads to a natural comeuppance. Either you go out of business, go bankrupt, or quietly fold your tent and start again in another part of the territory.

For very big companies, however, it simply isn't possible to quietly fade away. Too many people are involved in their success or failure and too much is riding on the ongoing existence of such an enterprise. This is even more true of countries.

There is a long history of nations getting into astronomically high economic trouble. After World War I, the economies of Germany and Eastern Europe experienced hyperinflation (unbelievably extreme devaluation of the currency) so high that my grandfather, for example, was paid 13 trillion marks a month as a university professor. Argentina, the country where I was born, went through annual inflationary periods of as high as 8,000 percent! Germany not only still exists, but it is one of the world's major economies. Argentina is still with us. How did this happen? What became of all the creditors involved?

The Trump philosophy applied (this is how Donald Trump dealt with his creditors who had too much to lose if he failed because his indebtedness was too impactful on his creditors if he did fail). In other words, once the debt reaches a level at which it is a concern to both the creditor and the debtor, the solution requires collaboration and accommodation. That is the basic premise behind the multibillion dollar "workout" industry where people who borrowed money to build buildings that can now no longer support the mortgage payments are given new terms. Their financing is restructured so that the lenders don't end up repossessing the building. This is not a question of kindness and benevolence on the part of the bankers. It is the simple admission that a lender who ends up with more property than it can possibly manage needs to rethink the whole idea of foreclosure, repossession, and subsequent management at a time when there are no ready buyers as alternatives and the market won't allow anything but the most distressed sale. In the end, the only solution that leaves everyone whole is a total reassessment, and sometimes the foregoing, of the original deal. Clean slates are often the only reasonable resolutions in such cases.

However we got to it, America is now at a similar point with our creditors, notably China. At some point in the not too distant future, there will need to be a frank and candid sit-down at which both sides need to face the facts, deal with them, and get on with their collective lives. Both sides need to recognize that America cannot continue to support the existing debt without damaging our own economy, that a collapsed America is in no one's best interest, and that China's best prospect for its future is continuing to have the United States as an economic partner, market, and supplier.

The outcome of this meeting will be a "workout" or restructuring (in effect, a forgiveness) of past debt against the promise of mutually beneficial collaboration in the future—such is the result of the interdependence of global economics. This is precisely the same fundamental under which Greece and other European economies have been given second chances rather than being allowed to go under. After all is said and done, it is in no one's interest to allow a country to spiral into catastrophic bankruptcy. The mess is too great and the cost of the workout is usually lower than the bill attending revolution, civil war, regional war, or international war. This is particularly true of a country accounting for an enormous piece of the world's economy.

SECTION VIII

Planning for the Future We Deserve

WE HAVE SEEN THAT THE FUTURE OF AMERICA, or of any one American, doesn't just happen. It is the outcome of every decision we choose to make or choose not to make. It is the result of a plan we choose to create and work from—or not. We Americans are at this juncture in history because of the conscious choices of disenfranchised diligent optimists going back centuries—as far back as the 1490s.

We are the nation we are because the common code of the Founders enabled them to put together a workable plan for America's future on the reasonable assumption that subsequent Americans would fit the same mold. The fact that the documents that embody that plan are still viable is a tribute to the power of those pages and the role they continue to play in keeping America America. It is also a tribute to the consistency of the uniquely American makeup over time.

The documents haven't changed in more than 250 years, but our connection to the core of who we are has been stretched thin and become a bit clouded by events and circumstances that have cast doubt on our ability to define who we are as a people and a nation. The quality of our future depends on how successfully we tap into the values of the America Code that has defined our nation from the beginning.

Using the America Code to decipher our central operating premise (COP)—to participate in and contribute to each other's initiative—I offer a twelve-step program to serve as a guide to action. I also wish to direct your attention to some red flags and warn of potential pitfalls along the way. By using our COP to reenergize the America Code and by heeding the warning signs, we can achieve the future we deserve and are willing to work toward.

As I said earlier, Americans may or may not be exceptional in the sense that we are better or worse than anyone else. What we are, most certainly, is distinct from the other nations on the planet. So our future not only can, but should, be uniquely American.

CHAPTER 71

The Central Operating Premise for America

AS PART OF MY PROFESSIONAL PRACTICE, I help clients to get past their mission, vision, and values statements to something more practical—something I call the central operating premise for their business.

Missions, visions, and values are aspirational—they tell us what we hope to be. Central operating premises tell us how to get that job done. Coca-Cola's central operating premise since 1946 has helped it to become one of the greatest marketing powers on the globe. It has nothing to do with taste, being "the real thing," or singing on hillsides. For over sixty years Coke's COP has been to put a Coke within an arm's length of everyone on the planet. That statement tells everyone that Job One is distribution, distribution, distribution! Everything else, especially global success, follows as a logical consequence.

I have developed a process for getting to the COP for your personal or professional enterprise—or for our nation, for that matter. In applying my principles to our country, the exercise goes something like this:

The seven markers of the America Code outlined in Section II of this book are also the seven markers of America's central operating premise:

1. We are disenfranchised diligent optimists.

2. We are coded for individual liberty.

3. We are committed to association rather than consensus.

4. We are fueled by the principle of possibility.

5. We are governed by a faith in something greater than ourselves.

6. We are pragmatic combatants.

7. We are collective congenital amnesiacs.

From these markers, we derive three propositions that define the American Vision:

A. We value your right to be you, as long as you subscribe to the same rule for everyone else.

B. You are entitled to the space you are able to earn and define as your own by means of your own initiative and labor.

C. However much we may disagree, even if it means disagreement on almost everything else, we recognize that there are things we must find a way to do together in order to survive before we go back to disagreeing.

Distilling those propositions yields the central operating premise for America past, present, and future:

Participate in and contribute to each other's initiative.

CHAPTER 72

A Twelve-Step Program for the Nation

I BELIEVE THAT WE MUST TAKE SPECIFIC ACTIONS if we hope to get back on track as a nation and as a people:

1. Only accept the word "unprecedented" if supporting documentation is provided that covers at least the past 250 years.

2. Return clarity to the national discourse by repealing, rescinding, and rectifying the mandate of political correctitude.

3. Insist on qualification of the source before you accept a position.

4. Reward candor when someone says, "I don't know—but I will find out and get back to you tomorrow!"

5. Provide a basic primer for political discourse in America beginning with the notion that for everyone you think is wrong someone is equally convinced it is you who are wrong.

6. Realign the definition of entitlement with its original meaning—which is to say that we are entitled to *try* but not entitled to have.

7. Revisit the original intent behind the concept of religious freedom in America as an inclusive idea rather than an exclusive idea—all about separating the church from access to the power of the state, but not of God from man.

8. Stop apologizing for being Americans and embrace who we are—we are not as bad as some and we are better than many!

9. Remind ourselves that we are not supposed to trust government—not ours, not anyone else's. That is the reason behind separation of powers. That is the rationale behind our Constitution.

10. Never ask the question "What has become of our country?" Nothing happens by itself—people are always responsible, and they usually have reasons for doing what they do. To paraphrase a mantra from the Watergate era, "Follow the advantage."

11. Never ask "What can I do?" unless you're asking for instruction and willing to take it.

12. Quit taking ourselves so seriously but learn to take real threats to our nation and to our future more seriously.

Still the Beginning.

A Personal Journey — Why I Had to Write This Book

THIS BOOK LIES AT THE JUNCTION of my professional life, my personal life, and my personal history, none of which has been particularly conventional. This work is the result of a serendipitous instant of insight that coalesced the aspects of my experiences into a singular discovery and appreciation of the America Code.

Whenever people find out that I was born in Argentina, they naturally ask how I came to be born there. My answer: "Because Adolf Hitler became chancellor of Germany in 1933, Bolsheviks deposed the czar in 1917, and Juan Perón led a coup in Argentina in 1946."

My father was an officer in the Polish army when the Germans crossed the Polish border on the first of September in 1939. He spent the next six years in one of their prisoner-of-war camps under daily threat of death. Had he surrendered to the Russians then invading his country from the east, it is most likely that he would have been shot, I would never have been born, and this book would not exist. My mother and he wanted to come to America back in 1946, but the little footnote on the Stature of Liberty said otherwise; the one below the better known phrase: *Give me your tired, your poor, Your huddled masses yearning to breathe free.* That footnote strictly limited the number of immigrants allowed by circumstance and country or origin.

Instead, he, his brother, and a small group of friends who had together survived war, imprisonment, economic disasters, and more headed for as close as they could get to New York harbor at that point. Their ship entered the harbor at Buenos Aires, Argentina, in the latter part of 1946. Ten years later, my parents had to leave Argentina because fascism and totalitarianism ruined that nation, too.

My Dad traveled through four countries across three continents to give his children a chance to grow up in the fabled and fabulous land of America. From him, and from my mother, I learned about the real world beyond our borders, about how to put our history in context, and about what it takes to leave everything you know in the hope of finding a better place for your children.

When I am asked what I do for a living, I can either recount a long series of job titles and professions or I can focus on the core of what that progression has taught me: I traffic in understanding how people make decisions, why they value what they value, and how that affects and defines *what comes next*.

The America Code is the result of those life experiences. Because of my personal history, I needed to understand why I in particular, and immigrants in general, love this country so intensely and why we feel at home here so much more than "back there." Thanks to my professional work, and the Index of What Matters Most™, I was finally able to decode what makes America America and Americans Americans.

Doing so at a moment in time when my beloved chosen country might benefit from this wisdom was the final catalyst that made this book both possible and necessary.

Thank you for sharing the moment and the insights.

ENDNOTES

1. Jack P. Greene and J. R. Pole, *A Companion to the American Revolution* (Wiley-Black-well, 2003),
   p. 328.

2. John Ferling, "Myths of the American Revolution: A Noted Historian Debunks the Conventional Wisdom about America's War of Independence," *Smithsonian.com,* January 2010, http://www
   .smithsonianmag.com/history-archaeology/Myths-of-the-American-Revolution.
   html.

3. *The Works of Julius Caesar* (parallel English/Latin), tr. W.A. McDevitte and W.S. Bohn
   (Harper & Brothers, 1869).

4. http://www.royal.gov.uk/MonarchUK/QueenandChurch/Queenandthe-ChurchofEngland.aspx.

5. http://pewglobal.org/files/pdf/167.pdf.

6. http://www.worldatlas.com/aatlas/populations/ctypopls.htm.

7. http://www.demographia.com/db-us90city100kdens.htm.

8. http://nationalatlas.gov/printable/territorialacquisition.html#list.

9. Source: U.S. Census Bureau, Population Division, Vintage 2011 Resident Population Estimates. Library of Congress (loc.gov).

10. http://www.aga.org/SiteCollectionDocuments/Newsroom/0906PGCPRESS.PDF.

11. http://en.wikipedia.org/wiki/Iron_ore#cite_note-3.

12. http://en.wikipedia.org/wiki/Hydroelectric_power_in_the_United_States.

13. Betsy Maestro, *Coming to America: The Story of Immigration* (Scholastic Press, 1996).

14. Ralph Keyes, *The Quote Verifier: Who Said What, Where, and When* (St. Martin's Griffin, 2006).

15. US Census, 2000.

16. http://middleeast.about.com/od/glossary/g/me090314.htm.

17. The National Bureau of Economic Research (NBER) is an American private nonprofit research organization "committed to undertaking and disseminating unbiased economic research among public policymakers, business professionals, and the academic community." The NBER is well known for providing start and end dates for recessions in the United States. The NBER is the largest economics research organization in the United States. Many of the American winners of the Nobel Prize

in Economics were NBER Research Associates. Many of the chairs of the Council of Economic Advisers have also been NBER Research Associates, including the former NBER president and Harvard professor, Martin Feldstein.

18. Thomas L. Friedman and Michael Mandelbaum, *That Used to Be Us: How America Fell Behind in the World It Invented and How We Can Come Back* (Farrar, Straus and Giroux, 2011).

19. George Santayana, *Reason in Common Sense,* vol. 1 of *The Life of Reason* (1905).

www.ingramcontent.com/pod-product-compliance
Lightning Source LLC
Chambersburg PA
CBHW081654270326
41933CB00017B/3162